Mekail Ahmed

Zakat for Social Development and Empowerment

Mekail Ahmed

Zakat for Social Development and Empowerment

To transform today's beneficiaries into tomorrow's benefactors

Noor Publishing

Publisher:
Noor Publishing
is a trademark of
Dodo Books Indian Ocean Ltd., member of the OmniScriptum S.R.L Publishing group
str. A.Russo 15, of. 61, Chisinau-2068, Republic of Moldova Europe
Printed at: see last page
ISBN: 978-620-3-85833-4

Zakat for Social Development and Empowerment

(To transform today's beneficiaries into tomorrow's benefactors)

Md. Mekail Ahmed

Table of Contents

Chapter 1 Introduction

Zakat Definition

Zakat literally means development acceleration. It may also mean either designation, purification, and invocation, or commendation. It is a commandment of Allah, and one must carry out every able-bodied Muslim's share. Every year, it is part of their personal wealth and property to benefit the poor of their society. While it is voluntary for a good Muslim to perform obligatory charity on the day of judgment, he or she would be held to account for zakat.

It is only through the charitable loans without any collateral and interest that zakat grants assistance to the needy community. It is one of the most important Islamic principles: charity to the poor. According to Islamic precept, a morally obligated person is obliged to give charity. According to Islamic doctrine, wealth is something that God would bestow upon those who are willing to distribute with love. People give zakat because they wish to show gratitude to the Glorious and how appreciative they are, and so this scheme is based on ethical behavior.

One of the five pillars of Islam is zakat, which involves giving of alms to the poor. It is a matter of faith for Muslims to pay back the poor and the needy, who have nothing. Muslims that have a sufficient amount of capital at a certain time period must donate part of their surplus. Islamic law is explicit in this regard Because of the Quran's laws, zakat is an act of voluntary charity; it cannot be considered a charity in the truest sense of the word. In the Quran, it is made clear that there is a duty and given instructions on how to follow the obligation. To properly carry out the obligation of zakat, a Muslim must both calculate and pick deserving recipients.

Abd Allah ibn 'Umar (RA) reports that the Prophet (ﷺ) said: *"Islam is based on five (principles): To testify that none has the right to be worshiped but Allah and Muhammad is Allah's Apostle, to offer the prayers dutifully and perfectly, to pay Zakat, to perform Hajj and to observe fast during the month of Ramadan." (Sahih al Bukhari)*

According to Islamic tradition, zakat (obligatory charity) is one of the Five Foundations, and that's why it's an obligation (fard). When zakat is over, it must be done by everyone, and not at the will of the person. If that were so, then only faithful people would be found doing it.

Zakat has a significant effect on making people fair. Zakat (charity) is an expression of Allah's commitment to provide for social and economic needs. Therefore, to create and to keep in place a civilization, one must grasp the value of zakat. It is impossible to be creative in an Islamic society without zakat activities. This is corroborated in the Hadith, where eight people qualify for a share of the value of zakat.

Allah (SWT) says in Quran,

إِنَّمَا الصَّدَقٰتُ لِلْفُقَرَآءِ وَالْمَسٰكِيْنِ وَالْعٰمِلِيْنَ عَلَيْهَا وَالْمُؤَلَّفَةِ قُلُوْبُهُمْ وَفِى الرِّقَابِ وَالْغٰرِمِيْنَ وَفِىْ سَبِيْلِ اللهِ وَابْنِ السَّبِيْلِ فَرِيْضَةً مِّنَ اللهِ وَاللهُ عَلِيْمٌ حَكِيْمٌ

"The alms are only for the Fuqara' (the poor), and Al-Masakin (the needy) and those employed to collect (the funds); and to attract the hearts of those who have been inclined (towards Islam); and to free the captives; and for those in debt; and for Allah's Cause, and for the wayfarer (a traveler who is cut off from everything); a duty imposed by Allah. Moreover, Allah is All-Knower, All-Wise." [Al-Quran 9:60]

يَسْـَٔلُوْنَكَ مَاذَا يُنْفِقُوْنَ ۗ قُلْ مَآ أَنْفَقْتُمْ مِنْ خَيْرٍ فَلِلْوَالِدَيْنِ وَالْأَقْرَبِيْنَ وَالْيَتٰمٰى وَالْمَسٰكِيْنِ وَابْنِ السَّبِيْلِ وَمَا تَفْعَلُوْا مِنْ خَيْرٍ فَإِنَّ اللهَ بِهٖ عَلِيْمٌ

"They ask you as to what they should spend. Say: whatever wealth you spend, it is for the parents and the near of kin and the orphans and the needy and the wayfarer, and whatever good you do, Allah surely knows it." (Al-Quran 2:215)

The zakat has great social benefit, but implementation of it to its logical conclusion is greatly dependent on the economy of the state, and the benefactor's willingness to use it, and the zakat is therefore at the mercy of the zakat organizer (Amil zakat). The foundation of Islamic economics is zakat (benevoluntary giving or charity). The function of the zakat organization is to arrange the divinely granted zakat and to convey them to the eight as ordered by Allah SWT. If the work is not finished, so poverty can only serve to foment more injustices and evils.

The above hadith supports the notion that malnutrition causes various symptoms, including criminal acts such as robbery, adultery, and murder, which is in some cases. as a result, Islamic society must commit itself to developing an equitable justice system for the underprivileged.

It follows from the above description that an Islamic institution, even if it is for the purpose of bettering society, people must bring positive changes. The fervor and devotion to fulfill our religious obligation is important, however, we must ensure that it is done with God's blessing. Zakat is a mandatory practice for all Muslims, regardless of whether it is a human or heavenly obligation. Similarly, it can be said that a Muslim who did not perform jihad is not a proper Muslim.

Zakat is an amount of funds and valuables that have met the standards of hauling and allocation, as well as contribution to stock. Zakat is one of the pillars of Islam's important social activities that each member of the faith must perform. Zakat is a sort of a sin against the property, which exculpates the spirit from hoarding, almsgiving, and contributes to the economy by separating property from the needs of the society, elevating the well-to-doership, and the global equality (Rahim & Hanani, 2014; Syahrullah & Ulfah, 2016).

Narrated by Ibn `Abbas (R.A.):

"A delegation of the tribe of `Abdul Qais came to the Prophet (ﷺ and said," O Allah's Messenger (ﷺ We are from the tribe of Rabi`a, and the infidels of the tribe of Mudar stands between us and you; so we cannot come to you except during the Sacred Months. Please order us to do something (religious deeds) which we may carry out and also invite to it our people whom we have left behind. " The Prophet (pbuh) said, "I order you to do four things and forbid you four others: (I order you) to have faith in Allah, and confess that none has the right to be worshipped but Allah, (and the Prophet (ﷺ gestured with his hand like this (ie one knot) and to offer prayers perfectly and to pay the Zakat, and to pay onefifth of the booty in Allah's Cause. And I forbid you to use Dubba." (Sahih al-Bukhari . 1397)

Narrated by Jarir bin Abdullah (R.A.):

"I gave the pledge of allegiance to the Prophet (ﷺ) for offering prayer perfectly, giving Zakat, and giving good advice to every Muslim." (Sahih al-Bukhari . 1401)

Sadaqah is a type of social and economic worship that is beneficial to the lower and middle classes. With proper zakat management, we can expect fair distribution of profits. Zakat is based on the word in Arabic that has the meanings of "cleansepurity" as well as "increase" (Siddiqi, 1968, p. 28; Mannan, 1986; Zayas, 2003). According to Ataina and Achmad (2010, p. 352), growth in worldly possessions as well as religious standing may be the reward that comes from payment in the land of zakat. In addition, 'Zakah' is stated in the Qur'an with other words, more literal, meanings such as 'compassionate' and 'mercy', both of which signify the sense of "relief" (Hairunnizam & Radiah, 2010; p. 462).

This will meet the requirements that have been laid out by syara in regard to obtain the money stipulated by syara to spend a certain type of money (Lembaga Zakat Selangor, 2010). There are two basic forms of Zakat: zakat al-Fitr, or zakat of need, and also zakat wealth.

Narrated by Abu Huraira (R.A.):

The Prophet (ﷺ) said, "The Hour (Day of Judgment) will not be established till your wealth increases so much so that one will be worried, for no one will accept his Zakat and the person to whom he will give it will reply , 'I am not in need of it.'" (Sahih al- Bukhari. 1412)

Narrated by Ibn `Abbas (R.A.):

The Prophet (ﷺ) sent Mu`adh to Yemen and said, "Invite the people to testify that none has the right to be worshipped but Allah and I am Allah's Messenger (ﷺ) and if they obey you to do so, then teach them that Allah has enjoined on them five prayers in every day and night (in twenty-four hours), and if they obey you to do so, then teach them that Allah has made it obligatory for them to pay the Zakat from their property and it is to be taken from the wealthy among them and given to the poor. " (Sahih al- Bukhari. 1395)

Narrated by Abu Huraira (R.A.):

The Prophet (pbuh) said, "Seven people will be shaded by Allah under His shade on the day when there will be no shade except His. They are: (1) a just ruler; (2) a young man who has been brought up in the worship of Allah, (ie worship Allah

(Alone) sincerely from his his), (3) a childhood man whose heart is attached to the mosque (who offers the five compulsory congregational prayers in the mosque); (4) two persons who love each other only for Allah's sake and they meet and part in Allah's cause only; (5) a man who refuses the call of a charming woman of noble birth for an illegal sexual intercourse with her and says: I am afraid of Allah; (6) A person who practices charity so secretly that his left hand does not know what his right hand has given (ie nobody knows how much he has given in charity).(7) a person who remembers Allah in seclusion and his eyes get flooded with tears." (Sahih al-Bukhari . 1423)

Narrated by Abu Huraira (R.A.):

A Bedouin came to the Prophet (ﷺ) and said, "Tell me of such a deed as will make me enter Paradise, if I do it." The Prophet (PBUH) said, "Worship Allah, and worship none along with Him, offer the (five) prescribed compulsory prayers perfectly, pay the compulsory Zakat, and fast the month of Ramadan." The Bedouin said, "By Him, in Whose Hands my life is, I will not do more than this." When he (the Bedouin) left, the Prophet (ﷺ) said, "Whoever likes to see a man of Paradise, then he may look at this man." (Sahih al-Bukhari . 1397)

Zakat is certainly one of the largest resources for the sharing of wealth in Islamic faith since it is one of the main reasons for economic development and well-being of Muslims. The word zakat is used in the Qur'an in 58 different appearances. It was listed in isolation 32 times and in combination with salah 26 times. Regular prayer is also an asset in the hereafter (Ahmad 'Atiyatullah, 1970). Besides salah, which serves as an Islamic rite, the scheme for wealth and equal sharing constitutes a just and trustworthy one. This shows the terms, meaning development, maturity, purification and calmness (Al-'Ayni 1972). Islamic scholars also argue that indigent and poor are the greatest recipients of the Zakat Award. The management must therefore ensure that zakat distribution is properly handled to achieve its objectives effectively. The mobilizing of the Muslim community, particularly the poor and the needy members, should be carefully considered to make the best use of the zakat fund (Nik Mustapha 2002).

Philosophy of Zakat

Abdul Aziz (1993) says that all classes of citizens deserving of zakat have their rights to earn. Zakat will first be given to those who are poor and vulnerable if categories do not have the need for it. This implies that the funds must be distributed to support the people receiving the zakat in some way. According to Monzer Khaf (1999), zakat is a means to get rid of poverty for the Muslim community. In addition, zakat seeks to help the impoverished by adding more money to their income. For those that need more help, there are several categories to choose from.

Muhamad Abdul Munaim (1997) maintains that the obligation in four objectives: to eradicate poverty, to implement justice, to create unity based on love, brotherhood, and family, and to improve the quality of life. Additionally, Husein (2003) maintains that the functions of zakat include creating not only an improved quality of life for the disadvantaged but also providing resources for the active members of society. The gift of zakat provides immediate comfort to those who get it, but it encourages them to obtain tools and equipment that will allow them to sustain themselves as well.

Shiekh Mahmud Shaltut included it in his book Islam, Doctrine and Law, under the heading "Zakah, A Principal Religious Pillar."

"In spite of my belief that theoretical differences are indications of thinking vitality and flexibility of the system that accommodates such differences, I feel uneasy when I see the range of difference among the schools of thought on the application of this obligation of zakah, as it is exposed in the books of jurisdiction and injunctions. This obligation of zakah, that is usually associated with prayer ought to be, like prayers, commonly understood. In prayers we see not much room for differences - just five prayers in the day and night. Unlike prayers, we observe that even the ratio, the exemption, the kinds of wealth that are zakatable are subject to differences among scholars. Such differences have serious implications for muslims at large when it comes to their application of the Islamic obligation of zakah. For example, some scholars consider the wealth of children and insane individals zakatable, others don't. Some scholars consider all agricultural products zakatable, others restrict zakah to specific kinds only. Some consider debts zakatable, others don't. Similar differences exist for business assets and women's jewelry. Some require certain minimum (nisab) for

zakatability, some don't. etc. The same kind of differences also exist about the disbursement of zakah."

Historical Experiences of Zakat

The Prophet's (ﷺ) administration collected and distributed zakat. There are numerous Hadith (Muslim religious narrations) traditions that show Muhammad (ﷺ) assigning a portion of the zakat profits to his devotees. He also appointed several deputies for the compilation and distribution of this, some of whom were corrupt in later times (Al Qaradawi 1973, pp. 749-53). Once he was appointed Caliph, Abu Bakr (RA) was obligated to maintain and return the appointment of all the Successors of the Prophet (ﷺ) including their stipends. Islamic leaders mention of taxes for one's companions was often directed towards the welfare of the poor: _"If the Prophet (ﷺ) were to die, we would no longer need funds, and the poor would be granted relief; but if the state were to die, all the funds would and the poor would still be supported."_

Abu Bakr (R.A.) said: _"If they withold giving (as zakat) even a (little) rein of a camel or a small baby sheep (that is due on them) I will fight them for it. Zakat is the due obligation on properties. By God, I will fight whoever discriminates between prayers and zakat."_

During the early years of Islamic rule, zakat officers went to possible zakat payers and collected the due amounts after having properly assessed their zakatable assets. It was evident how effective this process was on livestock and agriculture. During the Umayyad times, the tax collectors were the same officials who distributed the zakah. According to Umar Abdul Aziz, distribution of zakat took place on a regional level, to include within a larger area.

Like money, collection and distribution of zakat proceeded through the same channels in the time of the Prophet (ﷺ) but this changed with the introduction of the concept of AL 'Salah (which translates to God's coins). After the reign of Umar bin Khattab, merchants discovered a new way to amass profits, a new method of collecting zakat sprang up. He set check points on major roads, mainly those coming from outside the country, so that traders and consumers would both be paying the necessary duties on goods coming in, and made Muslims bear a portion of taxes going out. These officers were named al Ashir (Abu Ubaid

1353H, p. 595). During the early years of Islam, the collection and distribution of zakat was kept up by the government. Anything that didn't make it through the checkpoints was regarded as valuable because it was relatively easy to measure (Al Qaradawi 1973, v. 2, pp. 758-59 and Ibn Abidin 1301H, v.2 p.5).

How Quran Addresses Zakat

Additionally, it is stated in 82 verses of the Quran in the Zakat-chayat sections Sadaqah usually appears together with Salah, which is the testimony of faith. After this, a Muslim must bear witness that God is one. Take note of the repetitive focus and sequence of phrases in this explanation.

God's decree in the Quran:

وَأَقِيْمُوا الصَّلٰوةَ وَأٰتُوا الزَّكٰوةَ وَارْكَعُوْا مَعَ الرّٰكِعِيْنَ

"You shall [duly] establish the Prayer. And you shall give the Zakat-Charity. And you shall bow [to God in Prayer] along with those who bow [to Him]." (Al-Baqarah, 2:43)

اِنَّ رَبَّكَ يَعْلَمُ أَنَّكَ تَقُوْمُ أَدْنٰى مِنْ ثُلُثَيِ الَّيْلِ وَ نِصْفَهُ وَثُلُثَهُ وَطَآئِفَةٌ مِّنَ الَّذِيْنَ مَعَكَ وَاللهُ يُقَدِّرُ الَّيْلَ وَالنَّهَارَ عَلِمَ أَنْ لَّنْ تُحْصُوْهُ فَتَابَ عَلَيْكُمْ فَاقْرَءُوْا مَا تَيَسَّرَ مِنَ الْقُرْاٰنِ عَلِمَ أَنْ سَيَكُوْنُ مِنْكُمْ مَّرْضٰى وَاٰخَرُوْنَ يَضْرِبُوْنَ فِى الْأَرْضِ يَبْتَغُوْنَ مِنْ فَضْلِ اللهِ وَاٰخَرُوْنَ يُقَاتِلُوْنَ فِىْ سَبِيْلِ اللهِ فَاقْرَءُوْا مَا تَيَسَّرَ مِنْهُ وَأَقِيْمُوا الصَّلٰوةَ وَاٰتُوا الزَّكٰوةَ وَأَقْرِضُوا اللهَ قَرْضًا حَسَنًا وَمَا تُقَدِّمُوْا لِأَنْفُسِكُمْ مِنْ خَيْرٍ تَجِدُوْهُ عِنْدَ اللهِ هُوَ خَيْرًا وَّأَعْظَمَ أَجْرًا وَاسْتَغْفِرُوا اللهَ اِنَّ اللهَ غَفُوْرٌ رَّحِيْمٌ

"Yet you shall [duly] establish the Prayer. And you shall give the Zakat-Charity, and [thereby] lend God a most goodly loan. For whatever good you advance for your souls, you shall find [its reward] with God [in the Hereafter; yet] it shall be far better and much greater in reward." (Al-Muzzammil, 73:20)

Zakat as Special Virtue

The Quran, along with the statements and the actions of the Prophet (ﷺ) also say that no community or individual can be effective unless they do good deeds.

It has the capacity to cleanse the soul and bring the believer closer to God by eliminating one's transgressions. On the other, distributing the benefits of a country's wealth more evenly benefits citizens, reducing their discontent and prejudice.

"The notable Companion of the Prophet ((🕌, Abu Huraira (R.A.) elates that a Bedouin once asked the Prophet (PBUH) to instruct him in a course of action that would cause him to enter Paradise. The Prophet (🕌 replied: "Worship God and join not anyone with Him (in that worship)! Resolutely establish the ßalat-Prayer (in your life). Pay the Zakat-Charity (annually). And observe the fast of (the month of) Ramadan." (Sahih al- Bukhari. 480).

Narrated by Abu Huraira (R.A.):

Allah's Messenger (🕌 said, "If one give in charity what equals one date-fruit from the honestly earned money and Allah accepts only the honestly earned money --Allah takes it in His right (hand) and then enlarges its reward for that person (who has given it), as anyone of you brings up his baby horse, so much that it becomes as big as a mountain." (Sahih al-Bukhari . 1410)

Basic Features of Zakat

i) Zakat Eligible Items: Of all the obligatory charity contributions, zakat applies to gold, silver, horses, mines, and pasturing. From the viewpoint of commercial properties and company land, there are two views. One tax is imposed on the worth and another on the profits they produce. Zakat exempts possessions for the purposes of personal use, such as homes, beds, clothes, and similar; durable products for personal use, such as equipment and animals; other non-cash goods that are only used in the process of making final goods, such as houses and machinery.

ii) Nisab or Exemption Limit: The nisab is gold set at 7.5 tola is by law, and by equivalent to an estimated 84 grams of silver. Money in hand is equal to 612 grams of silver or 84 grams of gold, whichever is less. For agricultural cattle, the nisab is about 948 kilograms, but for the various other kinds of cattle, it depends on their age. For example, for sheep and goats, there are 40, and for cows and oxen, there are 30. If the number or amount of one zakatable object is less than the full quota, the individual must pay the additional deficiency; if the number of them is more, they are rewarded. An observant Muslim is supposed to give 20 grams of gold, 20 sheep, and 15 camels to charity.

iii) Rate of Zakat: Despite the similarity of the rate of zakat, all zakatable objects aren't necessarily rated at the same level as much as 2.5% for each of any of these three options. Pasture for cattle varies from 1 to 2.5% of gross food supply. In the U.S., it is about 5% of all farmland that receives irrigation and about 10% of all farmland that doesn't receive irrigation.

iv) Observable and Non-Observable Wealth: Things like Cash, Silver, and Gold can be hidden from the government to escape from confiscation, while items like livestock and produce cannot be ignored and recorded. In other words, Muslim law says that the state must levy zakat but even if it has to resort to compulsion, while zakat must be left optional for people to receive.

v) Usage of Zakat Proceeds: Only eight persons listed in the Quran shall receive zakat money may spend it on wayfarers, captives, those with past debts, and people going in the right direction of God. Right now, fourth and fifth-in-line positions are not important Muslim legal scholars have concurred on the position that the destitute should be given priority over the third-class students as well.

vi) Miscellaneous: During the year, if the amount of a zakatable asset (gift, grant, sum of money, etc.) does not surpass the nisab, then zakat is due. Fluctuations in the value of zakat are not included in the calculation of zakat. The zakat can be paid in kind or in monetary equivalent. Some, none, or most of it may be spent on the particular person or people in either case. Zakat can be given to the one who possesses zakat rather than the one who receives it and giving zakat to an organization to which one who needs it does not profit. Those who accept zakat are neither required to accept less than a full day's worth of meals, nor any sum over nisab.

It's been noted from the basic characteristics of the metric that there is a special tax on wealth that grows over time as well as idle money. For of category of income, the rate of progress can vary, depending on the amount of its support from nature. By contrast, the rate of non-irrigated land can be extremely high, whereas that of non-pastured cattle is very low. At the end of the day, the people it helps are always downtrodden. It is a good way to help prevent the accumulation of wealth and concentration of wealth in the hands of a few.

When did Zakat become mandatory?

God instructed his followers to pay zakat to assist those in the early days of the prophet's community. In the beginning, initial forms of wealth and sums were undefined. God spelled out how many and what kinds of acts of worship Muslims could perform during the first decade of the Islamic calendar, a decade prior to His decree that commanded Muslims to observe the Fast of Ramadan, in the first year of the Hijrah.

If one fails to pay zakat, what will happen?

Again, to pay zakat will allow you to receive material benefits in this world and divine favor in the Hereafter. Refusing to make the required offerings to the God is the same as incurring their wrath.

Narrated by Abu Huraira (R.A.):

The Prophet (ﷺ) said, "(On the Day of Resurrection) camels will come to their owner in the best state of health they have ever had (in the world), and if he had not paid their Zakat (in the world) Then they would tread him with their feet; and similarly, sheep will come to their owner in the best state of health they have ever had in the world, and if he had not paid their Zakat, then they would tread him with their hooves and would butt him with their horns. " The Prophet (ﷺ) added, "One of their rights is that they should be milked while water is kept in front of them." The Prophet (ﷺ) added, "I do not want anyone of you to come to me on the Day of Resurrection, carrying over his neck a sheep that will be bleating. Such a person will (then) say, 'O Muhammad! (please intercede for me,) I will say to him. ' I can't help you, for I conveyed Allah's Message to you. ' Similarly, I do not want anyone of you to come to me carrying over his neck a camel that will be grunting. Such a person (then) will say "O Muhammad! (Please intercede for me)." I will say to him, "I can't help you for I conveyed Allah's message to you." (Sahih al-Bukhari . 1402)

Narrated by Abu Huraira (R.A.):

Allah's Messenger (ﷺ) said, "Whoever is made wealthy by Allah and does not pay the Zakat of his wealth, then on the Day of Resurrection his wealth will be made like a baldheaded poisonous male snake with two black spots over the eyes. snake will encircle his neck and bite his cheeks and say, 'I am your wealth, I am your treasure.' "Then the Prophet (ﷺ) recited the holy verses: - 'Let not those who withhold (to the end of the verse)." (Sahih al-Bukhari . 1403)

Narrated by Al-Ahnaf bin Qais (RA):

"While I was sitting with some people from Quraish, a man with very rough hair, clothes, and appearance came and stood in front of us, greeted us and said, "Inform those who hoard wealth, that a stone will be heated in the Hell -fire and will be put on the nipples of their breasts till it comes out from the bones of their shoulders and then put on the bones of their shoulders till it comes through the nipples of their breasts the stone will be moving and hitting. " After saying that, the person retreated and sat by the side of the pillar, I followed him and sat beside him, and I did not know who he was. I said to him, "I think the people disliked what you had said." He said, "These people do not understand anything, although my friend told me." I asked, "Who is your friend?" He said, " The Prophet (ﷺ) said (to me), 'O Abu Dhar! Do you see the mountain of Uhud? ' And on that I (Abu Dhar) started looking towards the sun to judge how much remained of the day as I thought that Allah's Messenger (ﷺ) wanted to send me to do something for him and I said, 'Yes!' He said, 'I do not love to have gold equal to the mountain of Uhud unless I spend it all (in Allah's cause) except three Dinars (pounds). These people do not understand and collect worldly wealth. No, by Allah, Neither I ask them for worldly benefits nor am I in need of their religious advice till I meet Allah, The Honorable, The Majestic. " s Messenger (ﷺ) wanted to send me to do something for him and I said, 'Yes!' He said, 'I do not love to have gold equal to the mountain of Uhud unless I spend it all (in Allah's cause) except three Dinars (pounds). These people do not understand and collect worldly wealth. No, by Allah, Neither I ask them for worldly benefits nor am I in need of their religious advice till I meet Allah, The Honorable, The Majestic. " s Messenger (ﷺ) wanted to send me to do something for him and I said, 'Yes!' He

said, 'I do not love to have gold equal to the mountain of Uhud unless I spend it all (in Allah's cause) except three Dinars (pounds). These people do not understand and collect worldly wealth. No, by Allah, Neither I ask them for worldly benefits nor am I in need of their religious advice till I meet Allah, The Honorable, The Majestic." (Sahih al-Bukhari . 1407,1408)

Narrated by Abu Huraira (R.A.) The Prophet (PBUH) said, "Every day two angels come down from Heaven and one of them says, 'O Allah! Compensate every person who spends in Your Cause,' and the other (angel) says, 'O Allah! Destroy every miser.' "

(Sahih al- Bukhari, 522)

Narrated by Abu Dhar (R.A.)

Once I went to him (the Prophet) and he said, "By Allah in Whose Hands my life is (or probably said, 'By Allah, except Whom none has the right to be worshipped) whoever had camels or cows or sheep and did not pay their Zakat, those animals will be brought on the Day of Resurrection far bigger and fatter than before and they will tread him under their hooves, and will butt him with their horns, and (those animals will come in circle): When the last does its turn, the first will start again, and this punishment will go on till Allah has finished the judgments amongst the people." (Sahih al- Bukhari, 539)

Rewards of Zakat Payers

"For their patience, He will reward them with Paradise and silk. They will recline therein on couches and they will find neither excessive heat nor cold. The shades of the garden will be closely spread over them and it will be easy for them to reach the fruits. They will be served with silver dishes and crystal clear goblets."

"They will drink cups containing (soft flowing) sparkling water from a spring named Salsabil. If you were to see it you would find it to be a great kingdom with great bounty."

"They will have fine green silk and brocade and they will be decked with bracelets of silver. Verily, this is a reward for you, and your endeavour is accepted and recognised." (76: 12-22)

But how are we going to get this reward? The path is straightforward, but adhering to it demands considerable determination, as there are several paths heading away from the reward.

Allah (SWT) said in Quran,

وَسَارِعُوْا إِلَى مَغْفِرَةٍ مِّنْ رَّبِّكُمْ وَجَنَّةٍ عَرْضُهَا السَّمٰوٰتُ وَالْأَرْضُ أُعِدَّتْ لِلْمُتَّقِيْنَ

الَّذِيْنَ يُنْفِقُوْنَ فِى السَّرَّآءِ وَالضَّرَّآءِ وَالْكٰظِمِيْنَ الْغَيْظَ وَالْعَافِيْنَ عَنِ النَّاسِ وَاللّٰهُ يُحِبُّ الْمُحْسِنِيْنَ

"Be quick in the race for forgiveness from your Lord and for a Garden whose width is that (of the whole) of the heavens and of the earth, prepared for the righteous. Those who spend (freely) whether in prosperity or in adversity; who restrain anger and pardon (all) men; for Allah loves those who do good." (3: 133-134)

Our intention is what rewards us. We must make an intention before reciting each of the five daily prayers, and every decision we make incorporates an intention with a suggested consequence. Our total accumulation of intentions through time will ultimately grant us our eternal recompense.

The vast majority of our beliefs are spiritual in nature, in which we set a goal and proceed with our actions to meet it. Zakat, on the other hand, incorporates a physical aspect, as it includes giving 2.5% of our wealth above our personal requirements. This is accomplished when giving is done with the aim of pleasing Allah (SWT), in fulfillment of His commands, and giving.

This is a very challenging demand to place on Allah (SWT), but what are we offering in return? We are only simple trustees while we dwell on earth, we are merely keeping this riches which Allah (SWT) has provided to us to begin with. To be on the safe side, we are taking neither the benefits nor the burdens with us as we go on; rather, our intentions and deeds will follow us wherever we go, carrying us toward our ultimate reward. The delightful aspect of giving zakat is that it has no effect on our financial standing, but enhances our riches for the next year, as well as ridding our money of impurities.

In Islam, charity is a fundamental part of life, and it manifests itself in different ways, as Prophet Muhammad (PBUH) said:

"To smile in the company of your brother is charity, to command to do good deeds and to prevent others from doing evil is charity, to guide a person in a place where he cannot get astray is charity, to remove troublesome things like thorns and bones from the road is charity, to pour water from your jug into the jug of your brother is charity, to guide a person with defective vision is charity for you." (Sahih al- Bukhari)

Chapter 2

Zakat, Society and Social Impact

What is the Purpose of Zakat in Society?

The major themes of the Quran is for those who have been victimized and show compassion for those who are helpless. One of the Quran's major themes is social justice for those whom society disadvantages and compassion for the vulnerable. Allah SWT says in the Qur'an:

وَالْمُؤْمِنُوْنَ وَالْمُؤْمِنٰتُ بَعْضُهُمْ اَوْلِيَآءُ بَعْضٍ يَأْمُرُوْنَ بِالْمَعْرُوْفِ وَيَنْهَوْنَ عَنِ الْمُنْكَرِ وَيُقِيْمُوْنَ الصَّلٰوةَ وَيُؤْتُوْنَ الزَّكٰوةَ وَيُطِيْعُوْنَ اللهَ وَرَسُوْلَهٗ أُولٰئِكَ سَيَرْحَمُهُمُ اللهُ إِنَّ اللهَ عَزِيْزٌ حَكِيْمٌ

"As for the believing men and the believing women—all [of them] are allies of one another. They enjoin what is right and forbid what is wrong. Moreover, they [duly] establish the prayer, and give the zakat and they obey God and His Messenger (PBUH). It is these upon whom God shall have mercy. Indeed, God is overpowering, all-wise." (At-Tawbah, 9:71)

The teachings of the Quran and the Prophet's (ﷺ) example grow and become increasingly strong on the strongest and most secure land, such as the structure of zakat and other charities. Zakat is a crucial to Islamic culture and is active in both theological and social aspects of Islamic ideology. As well as necessary, zakat is a mechanism for the stability of the whole society. Zakat ensures equitable wealth distribution and thus has a vast societal effect. If zakat is considered an institution, it will build a mutual help or sympathy and the collective welfare system. Zakat not only establishes the rights of aid for the needy, but also creates a lasting connection between the recipients and those who provide it.

In Islam, every male citizen has the duty to work for his own well-being and that of his kin. In the event that one is unable to do one's duties, one's wealthy relatives help him. Charity links all Muslims by way of their common obligations to each other. Those who practice Islam place a responsibility on themselves to care for their community. When the act of worship is linked to collective responsibility, the principle of shared responsibility is known as takaful. Muslims come to believe that being Muslim means having duty to support one another.

Objective of Zakat in Society

Therefore, making charity easier for the eight groups (the needy, the destitute, debtors, etc.), as well as offering it to slaves, reconciling souls, and spending in the path of Allah – serves worthwhile purposes. The sole purpose of zakat is to meet the needs of certain categories of the community called "social insurance" and "social security" (Yusuf-Qard, 1999). Some types of social programs need premium and donation fees to get on an equal basis with those that aid recipients, such as zakat does not place participation as a requirement on recipients; it is charity to give money to those who are in need and receives funds from those that have more than they have contributed. When zakat first started, it had not relied on individual charity but on a governmental action, instead collected taxes and then distributed aid to those who needed it, it was in fact the first example of social security. There is no distinction between the deserving and the deserving poor, who get help from social security and those who get none. Zakat provides a complete package of services for those who cannot work and individuals who can work but prefer not to. Of the faith of an individual who is incomplete without prayer is of the third pillar of Islam. Zakat supports the moral structure of the society by including families in it.

In the act of giving, zakat fulfills an individual's duty to his fellow Muslim brethren. Zakat contributes to the needs of the willing and those who cannot support themselves. Zakat promotes tranquility and dependency security because it offers a protection to the poor and ensures the well-being of those in need and allows them to access to important public resources. Zakat is even more than just that it unites people through a feeling of trustworthiness, but it connects individuals through a feeling of provision.

Considering the Objectives and Common Benefits

The ordinances of shariah are meant for people while they are on earth, and their reward awaits them in the hereafter whether or not these benefits are needs. When the Muslim jurist Imam al-Shatibi argued that the various shariah injunctions could be ascertained by surveying the evidences, he pointed to a variety of sources to support his claims. Because shariah is a consequence of this previous concept, this does not only pertain to one concept or narrative. Al Shatibi said that with regard to worship the idea is that without finding any justification or motives, people would agree and follow.

Shariah's goals are to accomplish the people and to prevent damage, respectively based on this, the teachings of the Shariah. Malik and his followers held that the achievement of equity should be treated in the same manner as in Shariah. The key concept established by Ibn al-Qayim in a chapter is that religious rules can be modified as long as these conditions are considered. Before the text began, he found that Ibn al-Qayim was right in supposing that religious laws and doctrines adjust in order to the times and situations they're in. Shariah, however it may be applied, cannot be changed. The nature of the shariah does not alter. Ibn al-Qayim said,

"This is a great and very useful chapter; ignoring its ideas causes errors in understanding Shari'ah and imposes harrassments and unnecessary obligations, which anyone of sense can conclude that this great Shari'ah would not accept or bring about. Since the cornerstone of Shari'ah is to consider the benefit of people in both earthly life and afterlife Shari'ah is most just and all benefit and wisdom for people. In any issue whenever you go from justice to oppression, from mercy to its opposite, from benefit to harm, from wisdom to nonsense, you are going

out of Shari'ah. Shari'ah represents the justice of God among his servants, His mercy on His creatures, His shadow on this earth, His wisdom that leads to believing in Him and in the truthfulness of His messenger, (. It is the light with which people of sight can see, the guide with which those that are guided can find the truth."

'Umar as well as all Muslims has no right at all to abandon any texts in the Book of God. But Qur'an found that the common interest of Muslims at his time could best be served by saving those grants. He never thought to abolish the Shari'ah ruling about the share of heart softening in zakah when need arises. He simply refused to apply it to those ambitious individuals.

Another example of changing religious application to suit current conditions is that of Mu'adh bin Jabal (R.A.) when he was sent by the Messenger (to Yemen. The Messenger (PBUH) ordered him to collect zakah from the rich and render it to the poor. He also told him *"Take payment in grains out grain holdings, sheep out of sheep holdings, and camel out of camel holdings."* Mu'adh (R.A.) understood this saying to mean make it easy for people; take zakah out of what is available. When he found out that people liked to pay the value of zakah (instead of paying in kind) because it was easier for them he welcomed it. When Mu'adh (R.A.) stood in Yemen, he said *"You may give me cloth and fabrics instead of corn and rye as long as it is easier for you and beneficial for the migrants in Madinah."*

Faith Necessitates Feeding the Poor

Sura al Muddathir, one of the Qur'an's very early revelations, depicts a scene from the Day of Judgment. The righteous in their celestial gardens enquire of the disbelievers and liars who are engulfed in the flames of Hell what the motives for their punishment is. Among them are disregarding the rights of the poor, allowing him to be battered by hunger, nakedness, and pain, and turning their backs on him.

Allah (SWT) said in Quran, *"Every soul will be held in pledge for its deeds except the companions of the right hand they will be in gardens of delight. They will question each other and ask of the sinners, 'What led you into hellfire?' They will say, 'we were not of those who prayed, nor were we of those who fed the indigent, but we used to talk vanities with vain talkers and we used to deny the day of judgment."*

Clothing, food, and other needs are similar to feeding the hungry. In Sura al Qalam, God tells the tale of those who owned a garden and gathered its fruits at night to keep the poor and needy from taking charity on harvest day. As a result, God sent them a swift retribution.

The verses read, *"Then there came on the gardens a visitation from thy Lord which swept away all while they were asleep so the garden became by morning like a dark and desolate spot whose fruits had been gathered. As the morning broke, they called out one to another, 'Go to your tilthe be times in the morning if you would gather the fruits', so they departed conversing in secret, low tones, saying, 'let not a single indigent person break in upon you into the garden this day?', and they opened the morning strong in an unjust resolve but when they saw the garden they said we have surely lost our way. Indeed we are shut out of the fruits of our labor. Said one of them, more just than the rest, 'Did I not say to you why not glorify God?' They said, "Glory to our Lord, verily we have been doing wrong.' Then they turned one against another in reproach. They said, 'Alas for us we have indeed transgressed. It may be that our Lord will give us in exchange a better garden than this for we do turn to Him in repentance.' Such is the punishment in this life, but greater is the punishment in the hereafter if only they knew."*

Social Impact of Zakat

The tradition of Islam emphasizes the reform of those who are members of society. Each and every Islamic command starts from the individual and eventually ends up with the establishment of a country. Success is something that almost everyone can work at, particularly if they believe in, enjoy, and strive for. As zakat gives character to individuals first, it subsequently affects the community.

i) Individual Impact

Generosity

Human beings, from time immemorial, have always striven for additional property and wealth. In philosophy, zakat is a kind of movement from inside to outside the bounds. Instead of looking out for himself, he becomes a part of the race. He gives money to the vulnerable. It purifies avarice, selfishness, and frugality. The Holy Quran says,

وَمَن يُوقَ شُحَّ نَفْسِهِ فَأُولَٰئِكَ هُمُ الْمُفْلِحُونَ

"And whoso is saved from his own avarice such are they who are successful"(8)

The holy Prophet (ﷺ) has said: "Avoid from avarice as people before you were annihilated due to avarice(9)"

Sincerity of Faith

The practice of charity is called "Sadaqah", which is an Arabic word meaning "truth". Having assets and resources when taking into consideration the needs of the poor and the vulnerable demonstrates one's sincere confidence in the future. Because in the words of Holy Quran, *it is the characteristic of the hypocrites that "They come not to worship save reluctantly." (10)*

Narrates Abu Zar (R.A.) that the Holy Prophet (ﷺ) said:

"They are the losers on the day of Resurrection, by the Lord of The Ka'bah" I asked "Who are they? May my Parents ransomed to you!" He said, "They are the wealthy except those who spend here and there." (11)

Self-Purification

At the same time, zakat has the opposite effect on those who give as well as it does on those who receive. Thus, it reduces self-absorption and egotism in the one who comes in contact with it.

Obedience to Law

It brings responsibility and obedience. The Holy Quran says,

يَا أَيُّهَا الَّذِينَ آمَنُوا أَطِيعُوا اللَّهَ وَأَطِيعُوا الرَّسُولَ وَأُولِي الْأَمْرِ مِنكُمْ

"O you who believe! Obey Allah, and obey the messenger and those of you who are in authority." (12)

Divine commands, in a way, make an individual willing to obey laws and assist in his own cultural growth.

Special Financial Aid

Charity distinct from all other ways attempts at redistribution also aims to assist those who are unable to pay their bills. It also aids anyone who gets into financial difficulty regardless of their circumstances.

ii) Collective Impact

Islamic law originates from the family and then extends to the world. As zakat gives character to individuals first, it subsequently affects the community. As a result of the zakat is spent in this manner, it causes the following:

Social Harmony

In essence, zakat aims to cross the gulf between the less fortunate and the fortunate. We see that in market economies the wealth is increasingly concentrated, but the situation of the general public does not improve. Zakat was developed to ameliorate such social imbalance. The Holy Quran Says,

كَيْ لَا يَكُونَ دُولَةً بَيْنَ الْأَغْنِيَاءِ مِنكُمْ

"This (Wealth) may not circulate solely among the rich from among you." (13).

Social Security

Zakat works as a welfare system of social security for the poor. He who saves a little will save, and those who have a lot of money can save a lot. If they need money, they will get it as long as they can sustain themselves until the end of the day. Once, when I had fallen and injured myself, a homeless man approached me to offer assistance. I refused, since he had no other clothes but just a bedraggled rags and blood-stained overalls, and told him to wait while I dug in my pocket for my missing cell phone.

Best Check Against Hoarding

In Islam, zakat is levied on the savings and possessions of individuals. The faithful Muslim would rather give charity and see his wealth improved than see his wealth diminish after having made annual payments. The Holy Quran says"

وَمَا آتَيْتُم مِّن زَكَاةٍ تُرِيدُونَ وَجْهَ اللَّـهِ فَأُولَـٰئِكَ هُمُ الْمُضْعِفُونَ ۞

"That which you give in Zakat, seeking Allah's countenance, has increase manifold." 15)

This increases productivity and redistributes purchasing power because it takes money from the rich and gives it to the poor.

Circulation of Wealth

Zakat maintains capital flow, thereby benefiting the society as a whole.

"The holy Prophet (ﷺ) advised his companion Mua'az bin Jabal, while he was proceeding to Yaman "to teach them that Allah has made it obligatory for them to pay the Zakat from their property and it is to be taken from the wealthy among them and given to the poor." (16)

"Thus Zakat helps a lot in decreasing poverty. If proper Zakat system is established, the poverty will vanish away from the earth." (17)

Human Brotherhood

Zakat reminds people of the true meaning of charity and unity. Salat (prayer) and paying of Zakat are requirements for Islamic brotherhood. The Quran says,

"But if they repent and establish worship and pay the poor-due (Zakat), then they are your brethren in religion." (18)

Promoting self-esteem

Rich people must pay zakat. If they pay zakat, they are just performing their duty assigned by Almighty Allah. That has not benefited the poor or the indigent in any way. They must at least offer a fair compensation, for if they are left out of the share of paradise they will have to face Allah's wrath on Doomsday.

Narrated by Abu Huraira (R.A.) that the holy Prophet (ﷺ) said:

"No owner of the treasure who does not pay zakat (would be spared) but (his hoards) would be heated in the fire of Hell and these would be made into plates

and with these, his sides and his forehead would be cauterized till Allah would pronounce Judgment." 19)

That is why the zakat givers are themselves thankful to the receivers as they are helping to fulfill their duties. *The holy Quran says,*

يَا أَيُّهَا الَّذِينَ آمَنُوا لَا تُبْطِلُوا صَدَقَاتِكُم بِالْمَنِّ وَالْأَذَىٰ

"O you who believe! Render not vain your almsgiving by reproach and injury." (20)

Prosperity and Peace

Zakat promotes social justice by introducing financial balance to society's different strata. It lowers the rate of crime and terrorist tendencies among society's members. As a result, the whole society works together to promote growth and prosperity. The rate of unemployment is reduced and the risks of an economic crisis are reduced as income is distributed equally.

Major Social Issues and Zakat's Role in Solving Them

1) The Issue of Socioeconomic Disparities

There is no justification for extreme poverty in the Islamic society. A primary objective of Islamic society is to reduce the gap between the haves and the have-nots, and a major aspect of this goal is to supply to everybody the same economic benefits. According to Islamic law, which addresses these issues by means of economic and social distribution, Muslim countries distribute their resources as widely as possible in order to ensure that everybody gets a fair share. Saw earlier, zakat not only takes care of the poor and we strive to provide them with equipment to enable them to function, so that recipients become self-provisioning and removed from the category of the needy.

2) The Issue of Beggars and Begging

a) For many Muslims, demanding charity is distasteful, even when accompanied by extreme need. There are two major concepts revealed to his Companions by the Prophet Muhammad (ﷺ) as follows: First of all, work is the source of income.

Also, it is the primary means of sustaining yourself. Travelling is mandatory for Muslims in order to obtain God's blessings. Work, even if it is humiliating, is better than getting grants. Also, to ask unnecessary questions is not acceptable; doing so lowers people's self-esteem. According to Islamic law, Muslims must refrain from making unnecessary appeals for charity except for those who are in extremity.

b) One of the fundamental principles of Islam is to believe in the brotherhood of all believers. This can lead to a falling out among brothers because of money issues. Diffusing neighborhood violence and eliminating social environments' that encourage feuds are the responsibility of the entire society. Encourages amity and peaceful settlement with people in almost as many locations. Financial difficulties can need to be remedied by paying ransom, and in some cases can be handled by offering compensation. Of course, in this connection, "Zakat" also functions as a source of payments to those in debt.

Narrated by Anas ibn Malik (R.A.),

"A man of the Ansar, who came asking the Prophet (ﷺ) for financial help. Prophet (pbuh) asked him to bring a cup (that he had) to sell in the public for two dirham – one to buy food for the family and another one to buy an axe-head as an instrument (or capital) to get wood and sell it…… and after that Prophet (PBUH) did not want to see the man for ten days. After ten days the same person came back with ten dirham his income in hand. The Messenger of Allah (PBUH) said, "This is better for you than the begging that comes as a scar on your face on the Day of Rising. Therefore, begging is not permissible except to one of three. A destitute poor person, or a person with overwhelming debts, or a person who has to pay ransom or to buy the freedom for an accidental homicide."

3) Brotherhood is an Essential Objective of Islam.

Allah (SWT) Said in Quran,

لَا خَيْرَ فِىْ كَثِيْرٍ مِّنْ نَّجْوٰىهُمْ إِلَّا مَنْ أَمَرَ بِصَدَقَةٍ أَوْ مَعْرُوْفٍ أَوْ إِصْلَاحٍ بَيْنَ النَّاسِ ۚ وَمَن يَّفْعَلْ ذٰلِكَ ابْتِغَآءَ مَرْضَاتِ اللهِ فَسَوْفَ نُؤْتِيْهِ أَجْرًا عَظِيْمًا

"The relationship of brotherhood will breakdown, dispute and even fighting each other might be, one of this respects, due to financial matters. Reconciling differences among people and removing factors that cause feuds and may lead to fighting is the collective responsibility of the community and the entire society." (Al Quran 4:114)

Allah encourages reconciliation and making peace among people in more than one place in Quran.

However, such reconciliation may require financial sacrifices, since many differences arise due to financial matters; many others can be settled by paying ransoms. Therefore in this connection, zakat indeed offers a source for such payment under the title of the share of those in debt.

4)The Problem of Accidents and Natural Calamities

Allah (SWT) Said in Quran,

وَضَرَبَ اللهُ مَثَلًا قَرْيَةً كَانَتْ أمِنَةً مُّطْمَئِنَّةً يَّأْتِيْهَا رِزْقُهَا رَغَدًا مِّنْ كُلِّ مَكَانٍ فَكَفَرَتْ بِأَنْعُمِ اللهِ فَأَذَاقَهَا اللهُ لِبَاسَ الْجُوْعِ وَالْخَوْفِ بِمَا كَانُوْا يَصْنَعُوْنَ

"Islam attempts to guarantee each person in Islamic society sufficiency of sustenance and security from fear, so that each human being can devote a good part of his or her energy to worshipping Allah." (Al Quran 16: 112)

All the people in the Islamic state are entitled to food, clothes, and housing, along with proper health care and education under Islamic law. It was previously seen that the aim of the zakat is to help the poor and their families for generations. Amongst this other things, asset, those who are affected by misfortune are not permitted to leave, but are additionally offered financial support from zakat (Yusuf al-Qardawi, 1999, p. 564).

5) Problem of the Homeless

Islam places a high value on home and family, and wants everyone to have a place to call their own. Islam understands that adequate shelter is an individual and his or her family's needs have been fulfilled, because Allah has granted the fulfillment of both that to all.

An-Nawawi offers a rather descriptive definition of basic needs, which includes food, clothing, and shelter with neither parsimony nor profligacy. Ibn Hazm adds, *"It is an obligation on the rich people of every region to provide for all the needs of the poor in that region. If the proceeds of zakat and fay' are not sufficient, satisfaction of the needs for food, clothing for summer and winter, and shelter that protect from the sun, the rain and the eyes of passers-by must nevertheless still be provided from the wealth of the rich."*

There's no doubt about the importance of prayer and obligations to the impoverished population of society and nation. It is an Islamic bedrock principle to provide a correct balance between the wealthy and the poor within the society and to maximize wealth for all. One of the Five Pillars of Islam instructs Muslims to give zakat (Muhammad & Saad, 2016).

Is Zakat Considered a Type of Social Welfare?

Exactly. Zakat is, in effect, a nationwide welfare program. It has a strong mandate from the world of both religion and the market. Many of the game's laws, legislation, systems, and standards have been well-established for years. Although it is dependent on individual desire, it is by no means voluntary. In many ways, money has already been distributed fairly to citizen. As our resources are from God, they are provided to all human beings. Consistent with this emphasis, Islam incorporates an equal distribution of income and resources to meet the needs of all people. On the basis of one's abilities, one's identity, efforts, and approach, there are significant inequalities that arise. Worship [without] binding social regulation and manipulation, there would always be inequity in the distribution of wealth, and this leads to the concentration of wealth in the hands of a few. To respond to this, God commands people to have faith in Him.

Chapter 3 Zakat Distribution System

Theory of Zakat

Economists Peter Diamond, Dale Mortensen, and Christopher Pissarides were awarded the Nobel Prize in Economics in 2010 for their work in analyzing and modeling the theory. According to this theory, there are different types of imperfections or frictions in the real-world market, and these frictions result in buyer-seller mismatch. Imperfect or insufficient knowledge, slow mobility, and a lack of coordination are some of the causes of such frictions. It is, for example, expensive for both employees and employers to balance their supplies and demands. Laborers must devote a significant amount of time and effort to locating suitable work. Employers often need more time and money to identify and evaluate job candidates. As a result, both unemployed employees and employment prospects coexist for a time. Similarly, there is a disparity between zakat payers and zakat receivers due to a lack of sufficient knowledge and coordination. As a result, it can be difficult for individuals to recognize the qualifying recipients. To solve this, it appears that a collaborative effort is a viable option. Collective effort refers to a scheme in which an organization collects zakat from individuals and transparently distributes it to those in need. Zakat payers can now see where their money is heading and who is benefiting from it thanks to this scheme.

The Zakat Procedure

While zakat collection management improves every year, there are still many issues and discussions on the issue of the distribution of zakat. Among the issues which affected the performance and achievement of the zakat institutions are the difficulty regarding distribution methods, the distribution of zakat in qualified and unqualified Asnaf, the poverty problem, which remains even following zakat distribution, and the shortage of some zakat institutions while others have surplus (Mohamed Dahan 1998; Abdullah 1999). The zakat distribution issue is important because it can lead people who pay zakat to pay zakat directly to asnaf instead of a zakat. This will lead to a number of problems. If asnaf is paid by zakat payers directly, in particular the poor and needy, problems like zakat leakage and unequal distribution among asnaf arise (Sanep et. al, 2006). Zakat payers play a key role in ensuring the efficiency of operation of the zakat scheme. Anyone need to convince zakat to pay directly to Asnaf through a zakat institution. The zakat institution must therefore convince the paying zakat payers to produce zakat efficiently and effectively. That is the question to be answered by the zakat institutions. In order to mitigate their annoyance with zakat management, they have to understand the wishes of zakat payers.

Zakat institutions also need to consider how their role, especially on zakat distribution, can be improved and expanded. Zakat is an amount of the property Allah SWT requires of the individual entitled to receive zakat according to terminology (mustahiq). It's known as zakat, because it contains the expectation of obtaining blessings, cleansing the soul and using it with different policies to help society flourish (Al-Qaradhawi, 2000). In this way, the distribution of wealth is completed through market processes where only those with capital, experience and the possibility to enter and market are competitive and leave the poor outside the scene of numerous transactions involving goods and services they cannot afford (Rahman, 2002).

Allah (SWT) said in Quran, *"First, invite the people to bear witness there is no God but Allah and I am His Messenger. When they so bear witness, tell them Allah has enjoined the five daily Prayers. When they accept this, inform them of the divine commandment to pay the Zakat-Charity, which you shall collect from the rich and distribute to their poor." (Sahih al Bukhari No. 478)*

Zakat is required to be paid on surplus wealth that remains after a year, a lunar year to be exact. Zakat is paid at a rate of 2.50 percent of surplus wealth. Nisab is the minimum surplus of resources on which zakat is levied. Nisab comes in two varieties. The gold standard requires at least 85 grams of gold in a Muslim's possession as surplus after a year, while the silver standard requires at least 595 grams of the metal. Zakat is calculated on the excess of cash equal to each of these requirements. The Nisab amount of non-cash yet income-producing assets such as bonds and stocks is also subject to Zakat. As a result, calculating the minimum surplus of wealth, or Nisab, is crucial. After meeting all of a Muslim's necessary expenses and liabilities from his or her income in a year, he or she must own the Nisab equivalent of wealth. Only then is he or she obligated to pay zakat. Individual Muslims pay zakat, but the challenge is to make it successful. The issue of proper distribution arises here, and the economic theory of quest friction can help to explain the situation.

In Bangladesh, there is a long tradition of distributing clothing to the needy in the name of zakat during Ramadan. Such activities are in violation of the zakat standards and guidelines. The central tenet of zakat is to distribute the surplus resources of deserving Muslims in such a way that they help improve the living condition of the recipient(s) over time. The ultimate goal is to eradicate poverty and establish a more equal community. According to Hassan and Khan (2007), zakat funds will increase the government's taxation capacity by improving efficiency, jobs, and output. Based on Islamic principles, MACCA (Masjid Council for Community Advancement) has been introducing a poverty alleviation program by distributing zakat funds to low-income households.

What does the word "zakatable" mean?

Muslims who speak English create a word called 'zakatable' to refer to wealth and property for which one must pay zakat. When wealth and property is not subject to the holy alms of Zakat-Charity, it is known as "non-zakatable."

Things that are Zakatable

Zakat should be paid in the manner in which it is currently being paid, according to scholars. For instance, if it is paid for wealth, it can be given in the form of gold/cash, and if it is paid for animals, it can be given in the form of animals, among other things.

Narrated by Abu Sa`id (R.A.):

Allah's Messenger (ﷺ) said, "No Zakat is due on property mounting to less than five Uqiyas (of silver), and no Zakat is due on less than five camels, and there is no Zakat on less than five Wasqs (A Wasqs equals 60 Sa's) & (1 Sa = 3 K gms App.)." (Sahih al-Bukhari . 1405)

On What Is Zakat Paid?

Zakat is a tax that is levied on five different forms of material wealth:

1. Personal assets and resources

2. Trade commodities and exploited assets are two examples of exploited assets

3. Produce from the farm

4. Animals for sale

5. Treasure Hunting

What Are the Different Types of Zakatable Assets?

All possessions can be divided into two categories: zakatable and non-zakatable wealth. Muslim scholars have identified five categories of zakatable wealth for the purposes of calculating zakat:

1. Money on hand and in bank accounts, bonds, and money kept in retirement and pension accounts are all examples of personal zakatable wealth.

2. This is further divided into two categories: business zakatable wealth and personal zakatable wealth.

a. Company lists of products in storage are included in the trading goods.

b. Rented lands and warehouses have been exploited.

3. Agricultural Produce: This is also divided into two categories.

a. Crops grown on irrigated fields, with costs and labor associated with the irrigation system.

b. Crops grown on land that is not irrigated and is irrigated by rain or natural springs.

4. Animals raised for commercial purposes, such as sheep, goats, cows, and buffaloes, are known as livestock.

5. Treasure troves include buried and abandoned valuables, as well as natural resources such as oil, precious metals, and gemstones. It can be further defined as follows:

a. Discovered riches and hidden windfalls

b. Mining and oil

When Does Zakat Have to Be Paid?

When three conditions converge in a person's wealth, zakat is due:

1.One of them is a Muslim.

2.One's zakatable wealth reaches a certain level.

3.A lunar year passes while one's zakatable wealth remains at the bare minimum.

Is Zakat just imposed on Muslims?

Yes, indeed. Non-Muslims' wealth is not subject to Zakat-Charity, even though they are citizens of an Islamic state, since zakat is first and foremost an obligatory Pillar of worship, and Islam famously forbids any kind of coercion when it comes to accepting Islam as one's religion.

Is Zakat applicable to the wealth of Muslim minors?

Yes, indeed. Adulthood is not a restricting requirement for zakat, unlike other Islamic religious obligations. To ensure that everyone has an equal right to the money produced by the wealthy, zakat is exempt from age and mental ability requirements. A fact about zakatability, or the three conditions that must be present in order for zakat to be collected on wealth, is that it is the only requirement. This applies whether the property is held by an adult, a minor, or the insane. Zakat has to be paid on behalf of any child, orphan, or mentally disabled person whose income is equal to or greater than the minimum.

Is Zakat applicable to all types of wealth?

No, it's not true. Zakat is only due on zakatable wealth that exceeds a predetermined minimum threshold for that type of wealth. The threshold is known as nisab, which means "origin" or "beginning," since it is the level at which the poor's right to one's wealth begins. Thresholds vary depending on the type of asset. The nisab on currency, for example, is 85 grams of gold. Cows have a nisab of 30 cows. On grain, the nisab is 653 kilograms. It is exempt from zakat if the quantity of zakatable possession is less than the prescribed nisab.

Narrated by Khalid bin Aslam:

"We went out with 'Abdullah bin' Umar and a bedouin said (to 'Abdullah), "Tell me about Allah's saying:" And those who hoard up gold and silver (Al-Kanz - money, gold, silver etc., the Zakat) of which has not been paid) and spend it not in the Way of Allah (V.9: 34). "Ibn 'Umar (R.A.) said," Whoever hoarded them and did not pay the Zakat thereof, then woe to him. But these holy Verses were revealed before the Verses of Zakat. So when the Verses of Zakat were revealed, Allah made Zakat a purifier of the property." (Sahih al-Bukhari . 1404)

Who Made the Zakat Laws?

God's revealed concepts in the Quran guide the rules for measuring zakat on various types of wealth. The verses point to the Law Giver's timeless wisdom, as these concepts bear witness to the Quran's divine revelation. The Prophet (ﷺ), as the one who fully understood the Quran and carried it out, explained the concepts of zakat. Muslim jurists have rediscovered these prophetic paradigms and these foundational values for the believers on many occasions.

Who is qualified for Zakat?

Zakat is a religious tax charged to worthy people who fall into one of God's eight zakatable categories mentioned in the Quran.

"Indeed, [prescribed] charitable offerings are only [to be given] to the poor and the indigent, and to those who work on [administering] it, and to those whose hearts are to be reconciled, and to [free] those in bondage, and to the debt-ridden, and for the cause of God, and to the wayfarer. [This is] an obligation from God. And God is all-knowing, all-wise." (Al-Tawbah, 9:60)

The Quran outlines how zakat is to be distributed in detail, but allows Muslims the greatest amount of flexibility in collecting it. In the one side, this protects the rights of those who are in need. On the other hand, it accommodates natural variations in wealth stores, successful distribution systems, and diverse cultures over time and in various parts of the world. Trustworthy Muslim institutions collect and distribute zakat to those who are deserving and fall into one or more of the Quran's zakatable groups.

It's worth noting that Allah, Himself, defined the eight human categories of zakat disbursement for zakat payers and administrators, leaving none of this to the rulers, scholars, or the Prophet (ﷺ) himself.

Who is not qualified for Zakat?

If an individual does not fit into one of the eight categories, they are not eligible to receive zakat.

This involves six categories of people who are important to us, although there are exceptions within each of these types:

1. The wealthy

2. Many who are willing to work and earn money

3. Those who fail to operate are referred to as "devotees."

4. Those who are adamantly opposed to Islam and refuse to believe in it

5. Non-Muslims who aren't Muslims

6. Zakat payers' children, parents, and wives

Issues in the Estimation of Zakat

Since there is no agreement among the scholars on what may be counted as new wealth, there is an important need for a consensus on the concept of zakat products. Qardawi (1999) looks to qiyas (analogy), arguing that the rising wealth and forms of wealth such as bank deposits and securities as well as the emerging and increasing prosperity in the contemporary age, including financial securities and shares are zakatable (among those zakatable). Abu Bakar and others recommend that "piety's zakatability' should no longer be restricted to productive property; personal usage will suffice."'

That is why zakat applies to cash, inventory, real estate kept for resale, stocks, and bonds. Nowadays, development isn't restricted to farming alone; it includes other sectors as well. The key to development is the service industry as well as the manufacturing sector. Industrial production could be taxed in the same manner as agricultural production. At this stage, services income will be taxed in the same manner.

Summarizing, contributions to zakat should be according to the pre-defined percentage scales of wealth or productivity. As it is understood today, it is determined as follows:

i)2.5% above book value of keeping for trading inventory and above book value in excess of necessary trading inventory it is subject to a one-time charge per year on a specific date to claim.

ii) 5 percent of the production value or other than labour." The final stage of the operation or accomplishment of an income. Our time can be described as an extension of the terms we've employed in the previous centuries, with the modern day's equivalent being to collect zakat from manufacturing and service industries.

iii) Either 10% of any income derived from manufacturing or any other source is subject to a personal tax. The final stage of the operation or accomplishment of an income. A modern application of that collect charitable donations from self-type workers may be the equivalent of consultants, physicians, teachers, engineers, and lawyers. It can also include investments in securities such as stock shares, mutual funds, and real estate investment trusts (REITs) and funds.

iv) 20% free of labor and resources This holds true for treasure, which is collected without putting in any effort or money of one's own. the modern equivalent of that is to use for collection of zakat from income would be to invest the money.

The original theory behind the output tax was that the rain-fed land had to be taxed at a higher rate because it needed more investment. In addition, the zakat scheme can have a beneficial impact on overall investment, encouraging entrepreneurial behavior and enabling capital markets to be more liquid. We also spoke about zakat in our macroeconomic discussion as a stabilizing and counter-stabilizing mechanisms.

The Importance of Zakat Distribution among New Convert

He has provided zakat as a financial solution for those Muslims who have found their footing as stated in the Qur'an (9:60). With the help of alms, they reduce their social and economic hardships. The pious Muslim must first rid his heart of attachment to material things before embarking on a mission of self-sacrifice for the sake of Allah. Zakat serves as a social security, grants, healthcare, welfare, child-care, and transportation combined. Since zakat redistributes wealth, it has an impact on fighting poverty. Converting to Islam had become the most important decision of the new convert's life. They are exposed to a variety of stimuli that they are not accustomed to, such as being cast out of family, culture, and peers, as well as losing their work and financial resources. New Muslims may appear uneasy because they are unfamiliar with their surroundings. As a result, they need assistance and mentorship from the Muslim community to educate, encourage, and direct them on their new Muslim journey. They feel reassured and assured that they have someone to turn to when they have been warned about these problems and is actively assisting, educating, and answering questions. This is where a zakat assistant can help them both materially and morally, as well as provide support from a Muslim group that is feeling lonely and ignorant. Attempting to deal with any combination of these problems on one's own without help is a common explanation for new Muslims abandoning Islam. The need for successful zakat distribution becomes glaringly obvious as a result of identifying and highlighting these issues.

People who are in dire financial strait may end up going down the path of disbelief. Influenced and enlightened by people of other faiths, many people of different faiths will convert to Islam. Today's skyrocketing of the poor, low wages forced most of our poor to leave the faith. It is often worse for single mothers and females who do not have a job and have to contend with their husbands.

Rasulullah (ﷺ) said that being impoverished may result in someone becoming a disbeliever. We cannot ignore the vital importance of meeting human needs and providing for financial security in every human life. A human being in destitution is at the mercy of dissenters. The frequency of apostates has increased over the years, and they think it's at its peak among new converts.

Is it possible to distribute Zakat on a monthly basis?

Zakat funds will sponsor the poor person and his or her family if they are unable to work or do not have a daily income that meets their basic needs. This is accomplished by supplying enough food or funds to last an entire year, or by distributing it weekly if the zakat agency is unable to do so annually.

Defeating Zakat Rejectors

Those who failed to pay zakat are fined. However, if a party refuses to pay altogether, this constitutes a protest against the state and the religion of Islam. Although it is meant to involve conflict, it is acceptable when performed for the sake of justice on Earth. The rejectors of zakat, along with their lives and property, have violated the commands of God and His messenger (PBUH) by doing so. The question of opposing those who are against their interests is further reiterated by Hadith and the stand of the first of the followers is accepted by all of those who follow after them.

Bukhari and Muslim reported from Abdullah bin 'Umar that the messenger of God (PBUH) said: *"I am commanded to fight unbelievers until they testify there is no duty but God and Muhammad is the messenger of God, establish prayer and practice zakah. If they do all that, their blood is protected except by the due course of Islamic law and to God is left their reckoning."*

Muslim and Nasa'i of Jabir bin Abdullah have stated a similar saying. These statements clearly show that zakat rejectors should be battled before they pay.

It is possible that Abu Bakr and 'Umar did not have these sayings when they argued whether it is lawful to combat the zakat refuse without denying other Islamic foundations, for example prayer and fasting. Furthermore, there were fully rebels who retreated from Islam and requested false Prophets, such as Musailamah, Liar, Sajah and Tulaihah al Asdi and their clans. The historical stand was then taken by Abu Bakr. He rejected any differences between corporal adoration (prayer) and financial adoration (zakah). He refused to reduce what the messenger (PBUH) of God had previously paid, regardless of how small a reduction (baby goat and camel tether could be), He had not been weakened, given the risk of apostators invading Madinah, since some of the Companions had hesitated to fight against the rebels.

Zakat is the right due on wealth. By God, if they refuse to give me one baby goat they used to give to the Messenger (PBUH) of God as zakat, I shall fight them for it. 'Umar (RA) said, *"And by God, it was not until I realized that God had opened the heart of Abu Bakr to fighting that I knew it was the truth."*

Reported by all except Ibn Majah. (In another version Abu Bakr said "A tether of a camel" instead of a "baby of goat"). Umar took the words of the saying of the prophet literally to mean the declaration of faith alone is sufficient to protect the pagans, without attention to the essential implications of that declaration, without which the declaration itself is merely vain talk.

Consequently, fighting the rejecters of zakat has become a matter of ijma' that cannot be altered. Imam Nawawi said, *"If a person or a group of people refused to pay zakat, and resist the law enforcement of the state, the state must fight them, because it is authentically reported in the two Correct Books from Abu Hurairah that the companions, after an initial debate, realized the value of the opinion given by Abu Bakr and the strength of its supportive evidence and agreed with him in making the ruling on fighting zakat's rejecters unanimous among Muslims."*

The judge Abu Bakr bin al 'Arabi said about this claim, *"These are words of a person who is totally ignorant of the Qur'an, who does not know how Shari'ah rulings are derived, who wants to tamper with religion and whose viewpoint is falling apart on its own."*

Verse 103 of sura at Tawbah, The Prophet (ﷺ) must seek forgiveness for all who have generosity. But there is no one who can claim that the prayer of the Prophet (ﷺ) is confined to single purpose. This verse is applicable to all of all members of the zakat community. In the Quran, zakat has two meanings: the sanctification and purification of all who pay zakat, and the receivers. Scholars point out that purification, sanctification, and prayers for all who observe zakat continue until the end of time without interruption, and the reward associated with all other good deeds is lasting until the Day of Judgment as decreed by God and His messenger (PBUH) applies to every good deed of each and every time a good deed is completed without exception.

Denying Zakat Equals Denying Faith

Imam Nawawi said,

"Anyone who does not pay zakat on the basis of denying its obligation is considered a disbeliever except if that person is new in Islam or has lived all his or her life far from sources of information (in an isolated desert, for example). Then he or she should first be made aware of the importance of the obligation of zakat. If he or she insists on denying it, then that is disbelief, because the obligation of zakat is basic to this religion, without which Islam becomes annulled. That who denies this obligation denies the words of God and His Messenger (PBUH), and therefore is a disbeliever. This ruling is also established by Ibn Qudamah and other scholars."

Chapter 4

Zakat Fund Management

Institutionalization of Zakat

Therefore, the use of Islamic revivalism and Islamic economics increased the importance of zakat to non-Muslims, especially because the two combined to shed light on the practice of zakat, which is an institutional aspect of a formal national political system, but is also used to explain how it contributes to a state-based political framework. The traditional Muslim practice of zakat provided both personal charity and an important part of a properly working Islamic polity. Prominent figures advocating for the renewal of zakat during the 20th century included both religious and political elites. Zakat increased due to awareness of the religion and the news that religious teachings had been rediscovered. This in turn led to a renaissance of zakat-oriented organizations with only the aim of managing and disbursing zakat.

Scholar Al-Qardawi says that zakat is a state-run social welfare program and a tax administered by an independent government body. Sunni Islamic academics now can find greater support in the Qur'an, hadith, and early Islamic history for their belief that zakat should be a formal organization.

Scholars point to the existence of the category of zakat employees as one of the eight beneficiary classes mentioned in the Qur'an to support the concept of institutionalization and professionalization. The Qur'an is the most widely accepted source of Islamic law, followed by the Sunnah, scholarly consensus, and analogy to earlier rulings. So, since the Qur'an refers institutionalization, the existence of this proof is crucially significant. Another Qur'anic scripture instructs the prophet (PBUH) to utilize generosity (sadaqa) to purify the people's money and properties. Scholars say this is more Qur'anic proof that zakat should be administered by the state. According to some sources, Mohammed (PBUH) designated zakat collectors and believed that paying it was a religious requirement. Finally, considering the precedent of the early Islamic rulers known as the correctly guided caliphs, a formal governmental institution for zakat collecting is justified.

Zakat Institutions

For many factors, according to Yusuf (2000), the government should be held responsible for raising and distributing zakat funds. Instead of collecting zakat funds directly from wealthy individuals, the government would distribute zakat funds to needy and impoverished people, preserving their integrity. Furthermore, if zakat payers distribute the zakat funds themselves, it is possible that they would be influenced in a way that ignores the principle of zakat fund distribution. In a nutshell, zakat institutions have two main functions: collecting zakat dues and distributing zakat funds. These responsibilities will be carried out by zakat officers who have been appointed by the government.

Zakat Institutions' Organizational Structure

The structural strengths of welfare institutions such as zakat can be evaluated according to three criteria:

i) Governance and Management Structures: In all cases of management systems, a regulatory body oversees zakat activities. The supervisory authority is a government council, corporation board of directors and nonprofit trusteeship board. The members of these bodies are generally well-known individuals and can do their job skilfully. The organizational structure seems to be better format when we examine other areas of operations, such as accountability, adequate human resources, process consistency and cost efficiency. State, municipal, and federal governments all have to adhere to different rules. Decisions about new processes and those that improve performance generally include governmental procedures. Although the approach to management can largely be dictated by the scale of nonprofit organizations, the general principles remain the same. Nonprofit organizations can largely rely on the institution's size for their management procedures. The economies of scale would be able to support larger organisations. If the nonprofit organization is big, productive managers can be employed, workers with suitable expertise can be engaged and creative processes to increase productivity are introduced.

ii) Raising Revenue/Funds: essential problems are facilitated by providing information for donors to make their contributions, marketing and information, and building confidence. Zakah can also be automatically deducted from wages and charged at banks, post offices and the Internet, not just in the office of the zakat collector. Likewise, non-profit organizations are using various ways to advertise and collect funds for their programs. It is harder to boost zakat using these systems if the government collects zakat.

iii) Disbursement of Funds: To reach the poor, a minimal investment in personnel and services is needed. If these resources are going to be most effectively used to motivate citizens and develop ability, they will also have to be associated with social care agencies and other non-profit organizations to make it easier. To accomplish outreach to various population groups, corporations and non-profits have to set up a massive infrastructure. In other words, the job of alleviating poverty can be better achieved with government assistance from a well-coordinated policy involving different development agencies. Specifically, these monies will be given to various charities and non-profit organizations that serve the poor. This joint initiative has a greater chance of helping the needy and lifting them out of their circumstances of poverty. It serves the purpose of a good organizational structure and financial control and administration. More effective transfers of resources, however, can be accomplished by the government itself rather than the distribution of them to different non-governmental entities with a goal of ending poverty. In addition, it is possible to think of an effective method of running zakat institutions that would consist of two corporations: one that deals with zakat collection, and one that disburses zakat. Furthermore, there is a growing need for non-profit groups to work in tandem with the public sector to further address social and economic issues through diverse strategies.

Zakat Scale

The nations of 2013 gave humanitarian aid worth $ 2.2 billion to the Organization of Islamic Cooperation (OIC) (Stirk, 2015). Tithes or charity are commonly known as Zakat in Islamic faith (Haq, Ashraf, & Farooq, 2017).

It is based on the notion that every richness is God's and that the wealthy have a responsibility to help those who need it (Malik, 2016). Zakat is an obligatory charity payment of 2.5% (Ali & Hatta, 2014) of savings, to be paid to Muslim observers whose wealth above the minimum, known as nisab threshold. In general, nisab is low enough that a big population must contribute (Pollard, Datta, James, & Akli, 2015). Moreover the meal cost for one person is towards the end of the holy month of Ramadan zakat al-fitr (feast alms) (Atia, 2011). The act of donating is purified via zakat's wealth (Bremer, 2015). The main aims of zakat include providing poverty alleviation and redeploying income to foster harmony within the Muslim community called Umma (Atia, 2011). Zakat does not aim at eradicating poverty or creating riches and co-exists with taxation in broad terms.

Zakat can be expanded via volunteer contributions known as sadaqah and waqf endowments or legacies. Waqf is utilized mostly to finance the construction of mosques and schools, while sadaqah is limited. Some populations, like the Somalis, participate in Baho, a community-based philanthropic fundraising program (Pollard et al., 2015).

There are a number of organizations that collect zakat in industrialized nations and zakat can be privately contributed for people in need. In the U.S., the UK, Australia and Canada, Zakat foundations are founded. More than 1600 Muslim charity organizations are registered with the United Kingdom Charities Commission and 56 engage in foreign development or humanitarian aid activities (Metcalfe-Hough et al., 2015).

Muslims in several nations continue to experience economic hardship. They had to live in refugee camps because of warfare. There has been a continuing demand for funds from Zakat to help reduce poverty and to promote the welfare of Muslims. It will take a deliberate effort to enhance the management of zakat in order for it to run efficiently. Many Muslims also do not realize that zakat has the potential to aid the wider community in the long term. While many Muslims choose to pay zakat directly rather than work through management and empowerment programs, there are those who prefer to deal directly with charities rather than pass through the management and empowerment program. Another issue is that not all Muslim countries have zakat management entities that are capable of meeting the required standards. Thirdly, it must be noted that zakat is not applicable in all Muslim-populated countries. Zakat legislation exist in approximately one-third of the member nations of the World Zakat Forum. However, in certain countries, zakat distribution does have a substantial impact on the level of living of recipients. The fact is, many individuals are unable to determine whether the receiver of zakat is in line for it.

One of the efforts being made by the World Zakat Forum is to encourage members to immerse themselves in empowering programs, such as UNICEF and the UNDP, by collaborating with humanitarian agencies such as UNICEF and UNDP (UNDP). The money used to collect zakat has resulted in economic growth and community productivity. There are several different approaches to zakat management optimization, which can be done using digital technology. Muslim countries now have the opportunity to use the latest technologies in managing zakat (alms).

Unfortunately, since the world's Muslim population is still lagging in terms of technological competence, it cannot be assumed that all Muslims will be able to utilize the mission of digitizing zakat. While the globe develops rapidly, zakat digitization must take place. A team of zakat institutions is formulating a strategy for implementing zakat payments on salary direct debit. World Zakat Forum believes that solving this problem will support education and expand the amount of resources available in places that need support to grow their use of digitization of zakat.

Zakat Collection

In terms of zakat collection, the growth of zakat institutions in Malaysia is improving (Hairunnizam et. al, 2008; p. 805). Malaysia has seen an incredible rise in total zakat collection, with the country's total zakat collection for 2016 exceeding the amount of zakat collections for each province. Other variables, such as the rise in online zakat payments, are contributing to zakat collection development. Although most zakat institutions have started to use Web-based

Internet applications to electronically provide zakat information to the public, a few are still in the process of doing so (Shawal, 2009; p. 3). Through this type of marketing campaign, Muslims have become more conscious of the importance of alms-giving. Constant improvement in the reliability and accuracy of zakat collection has also occurred with the use of computer technology. Additionally, increases in zakat collection can be attributed to various causes, including increased access to banking (which lets people pay zakat online), an increase in the effectiveness of zakat administration, privatization of zakat institutions, and an increase in the number of people paying zakat (Hairunnizam et. al, 2008; p. 806).

In the Islamic state, it is the responsibility of the state to collect and distribute zakat. The *Quran says, "Take alms of their wealth and make them pure and clean."*

The Prophet (ﷺ) says: I have been commanded to collect zakat from the rich among you and distribute it to the poor among you.

In case an Islamic society does not exist or in a non-Islamic society, the local organization of the Muslims should make arrangements for the collection and distribution of zakat.

Wherever such arrangements exist, every Muslim is required to pay zakat to this organization and conform to the rates and the amount of Nisab decided by the organization.

Allah has made Zakat one of the pillars of Islam and has often mentioned it in the Quran immediately after the Prayer, saying, *"And perform Prayer and give Alms ".*

The Prophet (ﷺ) said, "Islam has been built on five [pillars]: testifying that there is no god but Allah and that Muhammad is the Messenger of Allah, performing the prayers, paying the Zakat, making the pilgrimage to the House (Hajj), and fasting in Ramadan." (Bukhari, Muslim).

يَّومَ يُحْمَى عَلَيْهَا فِىْ نَارِ جَهَنَّمَ فَتُكْوَى بِهَا جِبَاهُهُمْ وَجُنُوْبُهُمْ وَظُهُوْرُهُمْ هٰذَا مَا كَنَزْتُمْ لِأَنْفُسِكُمْ فَذُوْقُوْا مَا كُنْتُمْ تَكْنِزُوْنَ

Allah has warned those who do not give Zakat that they will face dire consequence. He says, *"O you who believe! Verily, there are many of the rabbis and the monks who devour the wealth of mankind in falsehood, and hinder (them) from the way of Allah. And those who hoard up gold and silver, and spend it not in the Way of Allah-announce unto them a painful torment." (Quran 9:34).*

Zakat Digitization Concept

Because of the direct benefits it provides to its users, digital-based technology is rapidly gaining traction in society (Rohim, 2019). The technical process of transforming analog impulses to digital signals is known as digitalization. Furthermore, digitalization is a socio-technical phenomenon that refers to the process of embracing and utilizing digital technology in individuals, companies, and society as a whole (Urbach & Röglinger, 2019).

Financial technology is one type of digitisation in the economic and financial system (fintech). Fintech development in Indonesia has been quite quick, and its expansion has led to efficient and productive financial sector practices. Furthermore, fintech has aided the management of various businesses, like zakat management companies (Hudaefi, Zaenal, et al., 2019).

In addition to technological developments, the realm of zakat has developed considerably. In the collection, distribution, administration and education of zakat, digital technology has been utilised. Usually, three platforms are used in the compilation aspect. First, the zakat's internal platform, for example applications, webpages, etc. Secondly, the external platform, a mechanism for raising ZIS money offered by OPZ partners. Third, the Center for Strategic Studies (2019) – Zakat National Commission. Zakat institutions have also made digital use of the latest technologies to strengthen the process of good governance, accountability and efficiency in the management aspect (Puskas BAZNAS, 2020).

Muslims still live under the poverty level in various nations. Conflicts impact them and they have to live in camps for refugees. Zakat has become a reoccurring concern in terms of helping the Muslim people reduce poverty and improve their welfare. There is a need for concentrated efforts to enhance zakat management to ensure effective operation.

To expand zakat's contribution, the World Zakat Forum invited its members to engage with humanitarian agencies like the United Nations Cholesterol

Foundation, the United Nations Development Programme, in order to increase their commitment to empowerment projects (UNDP).

Zakat India has used technology for alms-collection and distribution mapping by setting up an organization called the Zakat Foundation. Zakat distribution become more transparent because of the advent of digital technologies. Trust can be increased through greater transparency, therefore leading people to desire to pass their zakat through digital channels. Baznas has teamed up with various digital financial platforms for zakat payment in Indonesia. In 2020, Baznas expects that digital channels would account for 30% of overall zakat collection.

However, the problem is that not every Muslim population in the globe is technologically competent, therefore the task of digitizing zakat is not fully relevant. In the context of the rapid development of the globe the digitization of zakat must be carried out. Zakat institutions are working on a zakat debit payment scheme. With regard to that circumstance, the World Zakat Forum believes that the development of zakat digitalization will promote education and enhance resources capability in countries that are in need of aid.

Economic Management of Zakat

The Islamic aim of zakat management is to get the most favorable results as quickly as possible in accordance with Islamic law. As a result, it follows that any proposed method of zakat management should be judged in relation to that particular goal. While it is true that the foundation of an efficient zakat management is in the Qur'an, the status of the latter, who are responsible for promoting the operation of their own staff, is not explicitly stated. The contributions of the zakat house to both the selection and dissemination of that product or service are also considered valuable. Zakat staff jobs should be supervised by the ruler of the Islamic State. It is important to make sure that Muslims uphold this principle of their faith, as well as give the poor and needy their rightful share of wealth from the community's surplus. Abu Bakr (may Allah be pleased with him) waged war against those who denied the significance of zakat as a religious obligation. And because many of these countries still assume that zakat must be run under Islamic regimes, this could be the key reason why the distribution of zakat is limited to Muslim-majority countries. We must, however, remember that the collection and distribution of taxes must be kept distinct from municipal and national resources.

It is difficult to judge the effectiveness of the zakat scheme by applying different levels of confidence to it. It's the whole point of zakat operations to help Muslims fulfill this principle of Islam and aid the needy. However, if there is no confidence in the government a large segment of the population would choose to deal with their relatives themselves, giving money directly to the poor or vulnerable instead of the government

It showed the different views of jurists on the issue of whether it is possible to pay one's zakat if he is only responsible for any of the citizens or all of them. According to the al-Shafi'i'i in his new school, all zakat payers are in favor of just handing over the money directly to the zakat without going through the state.

In order to free the poor and give them the strength to better their own lives, Umar's (may Allah be pleased with him)solution was to give them the ability to help themselves (al-Qardhawi 1987; Sahata 2003; Shibli 2002). Essentially, the distribution of zakat benefits the needy and destitute by providing for their basic needs, and this is why he made a donation (Mustofa al-Khin et.al 2005). His opponents launched a civil disobedience movement to keep Umar (R.A.) from redistributing wealth to the poor and downtrodden. War was instituted to protect the destitute from having to share their wealth, allowing the well-off to keep their wealth. This war was also seen as a way to end poverty (al Qardhawi 1987 ; al Zuhaili 2005). It suggests that providing free allowances as a poverty-eradication strategy is successful. The reign of Caliph Umar (R.A.) shows how much good can come from charitable donations and how many people are indigent (al Qardhawi 1987; al Zuhaili 2005; Sahata 2003).

Islamic Economics and Zakat

Part of the Islamic revivalist approach to bring forth a new Islamic economy is the intent to re-establish Islamic economics. For proponents of Islamic economics, Islamic-themed regulations such as those that govern banking, finance, commerce, and taxation, combined with Islamic conceptions, are both realistic and also consistent with Islamic ideals. According to Islamic law, four economic principles can be derived, and one of these is a ban on usury (also known as riba). The Islamic tenet of zakat also encourages people with more to give back to those who are less fortunate. A third idea mentioned here is the discouragement of wealth hoarding and severe inequality, while another idea promotes trade. Islamic economists use historical examples from the early Islamic empire to demonstrate the core concepts and theories, and thus new economic theories and ideas are created as a result. Religious scholars, policy makers, and government officials began to pay more attention to zakat implementation because of Islamic economics and Islamic revivalism.

Allocation Function of Zakat in an Islamic Economy

The effective distribution of finite resources remains crucial regardless of the economic structure employed. A fundamental difference between capitalism and socialism is that in the capitalist system, materialism is only secondary to the four basic economic questions of: what products and services, how much to produce, who should produce them, and who owns and manages the resources and factors of production. The Islamic economic structure, in addition to pursuing positive material development, also establishes a path for spiritual upliftment by stressing the concept of monetary gains with that of personal well-being as laid out in Shari'ah law.

The Qur'an says:

وَابْتَغِ فِيْمَآ اٰتٰكَ اللهُ الدَّارَ الْاٰخِرَةَ وَلَا تَنْسَ نَصِيْبَكَ مِنَ الدُّنْيَا وَاَحْسِنْ كَمَآ اَحْسَنَ اللهُ اِلَيْكَ وَلَا تَبْغِ الْفَسَادَ فِى الْاَرْضِ اِنَّ اللهَ لَا يُحِبُّ الْمُفْسِدِيْنَ

"And seek in that which Allah has given thee, the home of the Hereafter; and neglect not thy share in this world." (Quran 28:77).

And when praying to the Almighty, a believer seeks the both the good in this world and the hereafter and enunciated in the Holy Qur'an as:

وَمِنْهُمْ مَّنْ يَّقُوْلُ رَبَّنَآ اٰتِنَا فِى الدُّنْيَا حَسَنَةً وَّفِى الْاٰخِرَةِ حَسَنَةً وَّ قِنَا عَذَابَ النَّارِ

"And there are some among them who say: Our Lord! grant us good in this world and good in the hereafter, and save us chastisement of the fire." (Quran 2:201)

A number of studies have shown that zakat has a positive impact on the economy (Rahman, 2003; Khan, 2006; Siddiqi, 2007). Increased aggregate demand, which pushes up the stock market, stimulates economic growth. So, it is clearly confirmed by research that zakat empowers both theoretical and empirical underpinnings for resource mobilization and allocation. Zakat strives to create productivity and stimulate demand in the Islamic economy (Faridi, 1983; Salama, 1983; Kahf, 1983).

Chapter 5

Zakat for Socio-Economic Development

Allah SWT recognizes Islam as a faith. Islam is a suitable faith to observe and practice in any epoch. The thoroughness of Islam demonstrates its greatness. Islam is peace in this world and in the hereafter, it is ibadah and muamalahh, it is aqidah and sharia, it is civilization and it is tamaddun. The Islamic Sharia was based not only on aqidah and ibadah, but also on positive effort in raising man's standard of living by building understanding in economic and social life. With the advancements in economic activity around the world, the dynamics of economic activity have recently increased.

Zakah is the world's first fiscal scheme to be remarkably complete, ranged from zakat payment subject to the item and their tariffs, the minimum land ownership cap that is not subject to zakat (Nisab), to property ownership period (haul) and to the dhimmi property allocation; (mustahik). If zakat is systematically enforced in the economy, particularly in the rule-based economy and in the Compellent Islamic Spirit, it would have significant economic implications. In the sense of economics, zakat has a broad, macro- and micro meaning, because zakat can be used in a country or in the general public sector of Islam as a tool for monetary policy, and zakat can play a major role in economic development.

Some scholars feel that zakat collection and distribution would contribute to micro and macroeconomics, including consumption, distribution of incomes and economic growth. According to Awad, Mannan and Chowdhury, zakat has major economic implications, such as total consumption, national investment, savings and total production. In the Islamic economy where zakat is used, society is divided into two income groups: the paying ones and the receiving ones.

A portion of their views is forwarded by the obligatory zakat community (Muzakki) to a group of receivers (mustahik). As a result Mustahik is unquestionably going to increase ready-to-use revenue. Increased incomes would also increase consumption and enable Mustahik to save on a long-term basis. On the other hand, zakat transfers would make it difficult for earnings and wealth aspirations to grow, leading to an even higher consumption. Zakat would increase consumption of basic commodities and services in particular and most likely move consumption from luxury goods and services to basic goods and services. The distribution of zakat to the needy and disadvantaged enables their income to increase. Due to their low richness and incomes, they probably buy basic goods using their zakat production and income (share). On the other hand, zakat will minimize rich people's incomes. Luxury goods and services must be reduced, since rich people are losing their wealth and profits. In several studies, zakat has shown a reduction in poverty. Patmawati shows that zakat distribution has an influence on aggregated consumption, but it is a marginal impact in terms of poverty reduction in Selangor, Malaysia and research in Malaysia, despite the fact that, technically, consumption of mouse drink is higher than muzakki. The restricted impact of the distribution of zakat on consumption could be due to the use of data on total consumption by Muslims and non-Muslims, whereas only Muslims are able to obtain the collected zakat. If a Muslim fulfills the eligibility criteria of the Shari'ah, he must pay zakat. A Muslim citizen must also pay a tax because the government may use zakat and tax in order to develop the country.

According to Nadzri et al. (2012), zakat was used as an important tool to fight poverty during the reign of the second Caliph Umar-bin-Khattab, and the Muslim world's poverty situation was dramatically improved (completely eradicated). Collaboration with other organizations such as NGOs, donor agencies, and microfinance organizations, according to the authors, is needed to enhance the effectiveness of zakat institutions. According to Sarea (2012), zakat is an accurate predictor of economic development. According to the source, when a country's people pay zakat, economic growth increases, and vice versa. The author also noted that zakat is a financial mechanism that aids in the reduction of inflation rates, the acceleration of job opportunities, and thus positively contributes to the resolution of social problems in Muslim countries. According to Mesbahuddin (2010), NGOs' microfinance systems struggled to hit the extreme poor due to high interest rates, while zakat-based Islamic financing systems offered instant capital to the poor at zero interest rates while also focusing on social justice and equity. According to Hassan and Ahmed (2003), the benefit of zakat is need-based and does not rely on contribution. Since the zakat system is based on the concept of unity among all members of society, it has the potential to have a positive effect. Raquib (2011) regarded the zakat scheme as one of the most powerful means of collecting and distributing large sums of money for poverty alleviation programs in Islamic countries. The author demonstrated that Islamic banks in Bangladesh conduct banking activities in conjunction with zakat and outperform the traditional interest-based banking system.

Socioeconomic fairness is one of the goals of zakat. There is no doubt that funds can be used to provide growth, education, and healthcare as long as well as meeting the stipulations of zakat (Hassan, 2010). It is therefore important to stress that this, since it is unique among wealth-distribution mechanisms. Zakat has proved effective when it is done according to the guidelines of Allah and His messenger (pbuh). It has the singular function of using compulsory donations and contributions to bridge the gap between the well-off and the needy within the community (Bakar and Rahman, 2007).

When economies are monitored using metrics such as gross domestic product and net gross domestic product (GDP and NEGDP), governments have useful measurements at their disposal. On the other side, these economic indictors confound the public, but when people donate to charity, the growth of the economy increases. Donating is important for two reasons: one, because it helps the needy, and two, because it helps to grow the economy. So to say, zakat serves as a kind of financial support to bridge the gap between social and economic problems in the Islamic world.

Inclusive Economic Growth with Zakat

It is a religious tax, traditionally paid by Muslims every year, which is collected from wealthy individuals and given to the needy individuals of the community. It has moral and social benefits and it purifies the hearts of donors who willingly give away their assets, for example, giving the best part of their lives to Allah so they may experience purest joy. It further narrows the distance between the "haves" and the "have-nots."

If the value of idle wealth, cattle, agricultural produce, and commercial properties exceeds a certain threshold, zakat is levied. The revenues of zakat are distributed to the needy. As a result, it relates to an efficient income redistribution process. It alludes to the importance of income distribution for economic growth in a roundabout way. There are better things to worry about than poverty because people are choosing not to have children because when they can. In classical economics, the production of goods and services generates their own demand for capital. This way of thinking reduces the relevance of income distribution to dollars and cents.

The population has been separated into three categories: the high saver in which everyone has spare money, the middle saver in which everyone has less money than they will like, and the poor saver or poor, in which everyone has nothing to spare. Zakat is a tax and its money is spent by the needy. The middle class does not pay and gets neither rewards nor benefits from it. As a result, each class of capital has been equalized that is equalized to compute the overall national production.

The Socioeconomic Infrastructure for Society

There is no doubt that the socioeconomic systems of the Muslim and the community have deep spiritual values that are a part of it, from the spiritual aspects, and those affect their individual and social conduct. Human contradictions and discrepancies are subsumed by virtue of an Islamic society's treatment of people based on these universal principles. The social and personal dimensions of Muslim life are deeply connected with Islamic organization. It is more than a religious experience, it is hopes, expressions of compassion, or it is just a sense of warmth and concern. His Islam will remain incomplete unless he pays zakat from the wealthy. Land was an especially important resource to Allah because He made us His vicegerents to take care of, and watch over. To put it another way, a Muslim is to be a "obligatory charity" for Muslims, for the needy, even if the land is not used, a public benefit is benefited. Capital, property, and labor are, in a way, partners to those who get zakat, the people who fulfill the eight criteria of zakat. Therefore, both economic and social well-being is being are secured. This equal right is recommended for those who are unable to participate in the process, as well as those who are prevented from participating because of lack of resources. This follows the law that no Muslim should remain in an absurd situation.

Socio-Economic Roles of Zakat

The idea of Islamic economic stability is rooted in the Shari'a. The instruments and processes of economic stabilization originate from the foundation of Islamic law. Economists limit the ups and downs in aggregate rates, earnings, and distribution, as well as liberate frontiers for productive use of resources like the aggregate. The attainment of economic justice and social equality coincide with each other. Consequently, the economic management objective must be to assure a sustainable and prosperous economy, but must adhere to Islamic rules and laws. In contrast, Islamic monetary instruments, in particular, and overall, have built-in safeguards against destabilization due to their lesser connection with interest.

Allah (SWT)said in Quran,

مَا أَفَاءَ اللّٰهُ عَلَى رَسُوْلِهِ مِنْ أَهْلِ الْقُرَى فَلِلّٰهِ وَلِلرَّسُوْلِ وَلِذِى الْقُرْبَى وَالْيَتٰمَى وَالْمَسٰكِيْنِ وَابْنِ السَّبِيْلِ كَىْ لَا يَكُوْنَ دُوْلَةً بَيْنَ الْأَغْنِيَاءِ مِنْكُمْ ۚ وَمَا اٰتٰىكُمُ الرَّسُوْلُ فَخُذُوْهُ وَ مَا نَهٰىكُمْ عَنْهُ فَانْتَهُوْا ۚ وَاتَّقُوا اللّٰهَ ۖ اِنَّ اللّٰهَ شَدِيْدُ الْعِقَابِ

"What Allah has bestowed on His Messenger (PBUH) from the people of the township, belongs to Allah, to His Messenger (PBUH) and (his) kindred, the orphans, the needy, and the wayfarer in order that is may not (merely) make a circuit between the wealthy among you." (Qur'an 59:7)

The Holy Qur'an states:

وَالَّذِيْنَ اِذَآ أَنْفَقُوْا لَمْ يُسْرِفُوْا وَلَمْ يَقْتُرُوْا وَكَانَ بَيْنَ ذٰلِكَ قَوَامًا

"Those who, when they spend, are not extravagant and not niggardly, but hold a just balance between those extremes." (Quran 25:67).

The Qur'an further states:

لَقَدْ أَرْسَلْنَا رُسُلَنَا بِالْبَيِّنَاتِ وَأَنْزَلْنَا مَعَهُمُ الْكِتَبَ وَالْمِيزَانَ لِيَقُومَ النَّاسُ بِالْقِسْطِ وَأَنْزَلْنَا الْحَدِيدَ فِيهِ بَأْسٌ شَدِيدٌ وَّمَنَافِعُ لِلنَّاسِ وَلِيَعْلَمَ اللهُ مَنْ يَّنْصُرُهُ وَ رُسُلَهُ بِالْغَيْبِ ۚ إِنَّ اللهَ قَوِيٌّ عَزِيزٌ

"Indeed We sent Our Messengers with Clear Signs and sent down with them the Book and the Balance that people may uphold justice." (Quran 57:25)

The two central pillars of the economic structure of Islam, namely, interest prohibition and the proper use of zakah (Yakoob, 2009). In order to allow the practice of Islamic economics, which emphasizes social welfare and equitable distribution of wealth, zakah is one of the building blocks (Ali and Hatta, 2014).

Narrated by Ibn Umar (RA): Allah's Apostle said: *"Islam is based on (the following) five (principles): To testify that no one has the right to be worshipped but Allah and Muhammad (ﷺ) is Allah's Apostle. To offer the (compulsory congregational) prayers dutifully and perfectly. To pay Zakah (i.e. obligatory charity). To perform Hajj (i.e. pilgrimage to Mecca). To observe fast during the month of Ramadan."*

Regarding the injunction in the Holy Qur'an, Allah the Almighty says: *"Alms is for the poor and the needy, and the officials (appointed) over them, and those whose hearts are made to incline (to truth) and the (ransoming of) captives and those in debts and in the way of Allah; and Allah is Knowing, Wise."* (Quran 9:60)

The fourth Caliph Ali ibn Abi Talib (RA) says: *"God has made it obligatory on the rich to provide the poor with what is adequate for them; if the poor are hungry or naked or troubled, it is because the rich have deprived them [of their right], and it will be proper for God to hold them responsible for this deprivation and to punish them".*

Al-Qardawi also argues that zakah isn't just a kind of adoration, but also that it's a privilege of the poor to receive the zakah proceeds that can not just guarantee economic stability, but mainly serve as an instrument to generate and redistribute wealth, alleviate poverty, and counteract social insecurity. The optimal distribution of resources in the Islamic economy strikes a balance, given its revenue and technological conditions, between the spiritual and economic imperatives of a society. Shafi (1979) describes three goals of the distribution of wealth in Islam: the right of individuals to follow Allah's blessings normally

according to their abilities, ability, self-will, and Allah's love.
Allah SWT stated in Quran:

وَابْتَغِ فِيمَآ أَتٰىكَ اللّٰهُ الدَّارَ الْأخِرَةَ وَلَا تَنْسَ نَصِيْبَكَ مِنَ الدُّنْيَا وَأَحْسِنْ كَمَآ أَحْسَنَ اللّٰهُ إِلَيْكَ وَلَا تَبْغِ الْفَسَادَ فِى الْأَرْضِ إِنَّ اللّٰهَ لَا يُحِبُّ الْمُفْسِدِيْنَ

أَهُمْ يَقْسِمُوْنَ رَحْمَتَ رَبِّكَ ۚ نَحْنُ قَسَمْنَا بَيْنَهُمْ مَّعِيْشَتَهُمْ فِى الْحَيٰوةِ الدُّنْيَا وَرَفَعْنَا بَعْضَهُمْ فَوْقَ بَعْضٍ دَرَجٰتٍ لِّيَتَّخِذَ بَعْضُهُمْ بَعْضًا سُخْرِيًّا ۗ وَرَحْمَتُ رَبِّكَ خَيْرٌ مِّمَّا يَجْمَعُوْنَ

"Allah is the ultimate Giver." (Q28:77 and 43:32)

وَالَّذِيْنَ فِيْٓ أَمْوَالِهِمْ حَقٌّ مَّعْلُوْمٌ

لِّلسَّآئِلِ وَالْمَحْرُوْمِ

"To enable everyone, the poor, the helpless, the needy, the paupers and the destitute too have a right to wealth and for the wealthy in the society to discharge their obligation and to a share their wealth." (Quran 70:24-25 and Quran 93:10)

مَآ أَفَآءَ اللّٰهُ عَلٰى رَسُوْلِهِ مِنْ أَهْلِ الْقُرٰى فَلِلّٰهِ وَلِلرَّسُوْلِ وَلِذِى الْقُرْبٰى وَالْيَتٰمٰى وَالْمَسٰكِيْنِ وَابْنِ السَّبِيْلِ كَىْ لَا يَكُوْنَ دُوْلَةً بَيْنَ الْأَغْنِيَآءِ مِنْكُمْ ۚ وَمَآ أَتٰىكُمُ الرَّسُوْلُ فَخُذُوْهُ وَمَا نَهٰىكُمْ عَنْهُ فَانْتَهُوْا ۚ وَاتَّقُوا اللّٰهَ ۗ إِنَّ اللّٰهَ شَدِيْدُ الْعِقَابِ

"And to avoid concentration of wealth in the hands of the few individuals, which is line with the Holy Qur'an." (Quran 59:7)

Furthermore, in view of the absence of empirical studies, Faridi (1983) believes that, in the early stage, the fiscal dynamics of an Islamic society depends on relevant standards and values relating to state allocation, distribution and stabilization and the models of conduct of an Islamic economic system, as dates for a theoretical prediction of the future.

In another empirical report, Hassan and Jauanyed (2007) conclude that the governmental expenses represented by the Annual Development Programme of the Government (ADP) have decreased from 21% of ADP in 1983-84 to 43% of ADP in 2004-2005. For Malaysia, 73% of the annual zakat collection is thought to be needed to turn the zakat recipients into non-poor Malaysian people. On the basis of findings from Malaysia, Ibrahim (2006) contends that zakat (almsgiving) decreases income inequality. He found that distribution of zakat decreases poverty incidence, reduces the depth of poverty, and does so for less money than any other method, it does. Firdaus, et al. (2012) put together the country's potential zakat capacity from surveys of around 345 rural households. In the study above, their findings show that zakat could add 3.4% to the GDP of Indonesia. Comparative results indicate that zakat has a higher impact on poverty reduction. Debnath et al. (2013), the success of zakat to end poverty in Bangladesh is evaluated by granting microcredit loans to people who want to start businesses is put into question. By applying PSM techniques, the results show that zakat has a larger effect than using microfinance schemes. In addition, it highlights that the zakat program provides greatly raises both income and expenditure for the recipients.

Zakat is very versatile. In the era of the statesmanship of Umar and Abu Bakr, zakat was distributed by the government. However, zakat was not yet provided in cash (In Usman's time, people were allowed to pay their zakat out in kind). Horses were exempted from zakat in the time of the Prophet (pbuh), but after that Umer (rta) included them in the equation. In reference to the traditional view of zakat, Mahmud (2001) maintains that it is versatile to an extent, because during a period of drought and famine, it was in effect collected from the poor and relaxed for the wealthy. By end of the twentieth century, however, zakat also imposed levies on forest products that were previously tax-exempt in both the Ottoman era (1980s) and the modern period (1980s and after). Thus, in a modern economy, a policy maker can maximize the zakat benefits by using this mechanism.

This is, of course, in spite of the fact that zakat was traditionally collected by governments in the past and is no longer now usually demanded as a duty that should be paid to them. The reasoning proposed by Abu Bakar, et al. (2007) is that Muslim countries do not successfully enforce zakat because of its noble objectives. Yusoff (2011) suggests that zakat (charity) must be collected and distributed by any Islamic country in the most effective and efficient manner possible. Proponents of the zakat scheme also argue that it needs to be formalised to boost the zakat revenue.

Zakat in Social Development

Zakat is among the year's of those who have obligations, which may be described as Sahib-Nisab, once in return if he is prosperous, or once in his life if he is poor (a minimum prescribed amount by Shariah, which varies for the different categories). It is founded on Islamic principles (9:60; 9:103). A number of examples in early Islamic history can be found in the practice of zakat, i.e., the process of raising and distribution. The main goal of this mechanism is to keep the economy operating at a constant equilibrium at the same time, while limiting the concentration of capital. A better life for all sections of the population is achievable through this process. Zakat is believed to be a way to help the poor. This system would ensure that everybody gets the basics of life. The main difference between zakat and other charities is that it stands a primary moral obligation, in addition to the ones which are more or less of a personal choice. Zakat is particularly useful for the economically underprivileged population. Often, this builds their self-esteem as socially significant members of society. People in this under the lower socioeconomic strata use their talents and engagement in various economic and social activities in order to promote their well-being.

The scheme of charitable giving in Islam has an independent existence, implications, and priorities. It is Said of the Prophet (pbuh) that charity will make a businessman a saint. As well, the creation of a civic group working to make social lives for the establishment of a group or organization. Salaries to the collectors of zakat will be managed in a financial firm. Finally, the system would be able to realize social and economic justice. Transfer of funds between the better-off and the poorer population is integrated into the scheme.

Many Islamic norms are outdated, but the zakat approach is extremely potent in sections of the Muslim society. It has been noted that in numerous Muslim-majority regions, such as Yemen, that the zakat system has a positive impact on the community. Zakat is a means of Islamic government policy as much as it is a charity. It is not limited to those who are currently residing in an Islamic state, but it is incumbent on all Muslims to comply with it regardless of where they currently reside. It is widely alleged that millions of Muslims are donating money each year as well as money under the threat of death.

Contribution towards Socio-Economic Development

Benefits to the individuals who are applying for this scheme may be denied, but it cannot be denied that this mechanism has the ability to support agriculture, education, health, infrastructure, and services in rural areas as well. Prevention of poverty is a good idea for the Muslim countries, as it is for the multiracial ones. Thus, the percentage of poverty among Malay-Chinese and Indian-Hindu households went from 25.8% to 23.1% to 9.7% and 10.1% to 9.1% between 1987 and 1992. Malaysia has the highest poverty among Muslims of any state in the world reducing poverty is the aim. All the zakat money will be placed in long-term assets and the rest in pocket money that could be liquidated for the necessities of life. In addition, they can buy and sell these shares as they see fit. The beneficiaries will benefit from additional dividend and stock-based compounding power. Some individuals are given zakat regardless of their level of physical capability in terms of food, clothes, house, and medical care, due to a lifelong illness like blindness, crippled, elderly, or without family to support becoming an orphan. Others can find themselves in this situation because of economic problems. This group has a right to dividends from the assets in perpetuity. For people with disabilities, there is often a benefit in obtaining stock instead of cash, so they may be able to handle their own investments. Everyone has the right to receive services, even those who are unable to function due to old age or sickness. Living wages of those who can't make it on their own should be replaced by transfers. Therefore, full effort should be used to help beneficiaries obtain a self-sustaining existence as soon as possible. It has been recommended that the payments be made in so that the recipients' self-esteem is not affected.

Nisab and its Role in Social Development

All forms of zakat could be paid with gold, silver, goods, animals, treasure, or produce in the early Islamic period. According to one methodology of ijtihad which holds true in modern times, as well as medieval times, salaries and financial assets like bond holdings, the jurists accept that today, as before it, zakat must be paid. Items in the owners' private homes, such as clothing, cooking utensils, etc., are not tracked. On the other hand, different school of thought holds that fixed assets are not subject to zakat as well. Agricultural land is thought to be untouchable by scholars. Many legal scholars consider other fixed assets like factories, for example, fixed assets such as machinery, warehouse and buildings as exempt from zakat. Some jurists believe fixed assets are an obligation to pay zakat. It has also been proposed that farm or agricultural product levy revenues from rentals be included in the assessment of zakat. Some jurists favor taking wages and salaries after loans and expenditures have been paid, while others believe that it should be after taxes are deducted.

The nisab (the minimum amount or quantity which places a load upon zakat) was ordered by the Prophet (﷽ and consensus (Ijma') from the legal scholars says that no deviation from this is permitted. The dinar-weight of gold is 20 grams and the dirham-weight of silver is 595 grams. There are, therefore, several similarities between the nisab for money, other financial assets, gold and silver. This meant that 20 dirhams was the equivalent of a US dollar in the early days of Islam. Gold is on the rise over the long term, and has fallen in relation to silver. Some theologist says that the minimum holdings of currency, as well as other financial properties, commodities, should be valued at 20 dirham of silver, while others say that they must be worth at 200 dirham of silver in order to be included in the zakat. According to some legal scholars, dirham equivalence may help to increase revenues for the needy. In modern use, the cost of living has increased greatly compared to the early Islamic era. The nisab for agricultural product is 3 bushels of grain or 350 pounds of produce; for non-staple agricultural products, it is 150 kg. While the food ration differs by form, livestock has a nisab. In the cases of camels, the number is five; in that of bovines, it is thirty; and in the cases of sheep and goats, it is forty. In the early Islamic period there was no knowledge of nisab for mineral or food products. For others, there is no stipulation in relation to minimum holding for mineral production; according to others, it is subjected to levy as long as production value is obtained in the year. In addition, the recommended rates of tax for different goods as well. The reduced pricing structure of 2.5% for gold, silver, currency, and merchandise applies in the situation. In the case of food stored agricultural produce, the charge is 10% for rainfall-irriggated crops and 5% for those watered. Information is detailed in the Quran on the application of the distribution of the zakat for all kinds of livestock.

For treasure it is $20. The specific placement of minerals in the Islamic period is not understood. Some advocates believe that mineral resource extraction is taxed at 2.5 percent, while others believe it is taxed at 20 percent. Liability results from properties being in your hands for one year or more. Almost all of our supplies are susceptible to it, but there are exceptions to the rule: things like agricultural products. In essence, zakat is based on the same asset during the year but zakah is based on each time a new harvest is produced. There have at times been suggestions that the fixed zakat ratio could be changed on different products. Such views, however, have been opposed by Islamic populations around the world.

An unknown rate of change for nisab would cast doubt on the type of ibadah, and could possibly introduce volatile and complex elements into a proper, dependable system. Additionally, it has been noted that even with invariant nisab and wide nisab-rate resources are still sufficient to alleviate poverty because the nisab rate is poor. There is virtually no one who does not contribute in any way to the tax burden, other than the extremely impoverished. Economists have found that each year, 3-4% of GDP is transferred to poorer parts of the population due to development in the area in question. In wealthier countries, such as the United States, the state's obligations would be greater than those of the federal government because it has far more power-holders, whereas in poorer nations, the federal government's role would be less important. Whatever these particular differences, the nisab-system of zakat serves to drive social progress in all civilizations.

Policy Recommendations to Mobilize Zakat Resources

i. Contrary to popular views of insufficient dependability in donation flows, zakat is reliable, sustained and could become an increasing source of funds for fund-raising institutions seeking to develop professionalism and to further boost their social reputation through efforts to foster honesty, accountability and good governance. This has been shown in countries in South-East Asia. The evidence has more mixed up in Sub-Saharan Africa's agricultural economies, where zakat collections have increased volatility due to the changing wealth in agriculture.

ii. In mobilizing zakat in South Asia and South East Asia, there is a significant upward trend. In Indonesia and Malaysia, zakat mobilization in two separate zakat systems has evolved steadily. In Malaysia, zakat is mandatory, but in Indonesia it is optional. In these areas, such as Bangladesh, India, Pakistan and Sub-Saharan Africa, growth patterns are more diverse. In Sudan and Nigeria, zakat is obligatory but is optional in other Nigerian states and in other studied countries. The average growth rate in Sudan for zakat has gradually increased by 19% annually. Zakat is remarkable in Sudan in absolute terms. It ranks behind Saudi Arabia, Malaysia and Indonesia at around 200 million dollars annually. It is however much better than Indonesia in terms of per capita zakat obtained.

iii. Malaysia and Sudan supply compulsory zakat evidence. Nigeria's compulsory and voluntary zakat countries have modest proof of mandatory zakat, and their results are comparatively improved in states such as Jigawa and Zamfara. The lack of a lively network of organizations at various levels may be a significant factor. The performance of voluntary zakat organizations was excellent in Indonesia, Pakistan and South Africa. Whether zakat is obligatory or optional, a decentralization policy appears to work.

iv. It is critical to incentivize zakat payment. When zakat payment is made mandatory and noncompliance is punishable by fines and punishment, as in some Nigerian states, poor enforcement can lead to low zakat collection.

v. On the other hand, the incentives for cooperation between agencies in Nigerian states have been removed, causing more uncertainty. When private organisations may receive zakat, zakat payment appears to be an appropriate deduction only on a par with different types of charitable flows. When paying to private collection bodies, the zakat payment on an equal footing with taxes on the state will severely undermine the income of state.

vi. There seems to be no clear case that the definition of zakat liable assets and methods used in estimating their liability is standardized and globally acceptable. Since Islamic societies traditionally have many madhabs and think-tanks, zakat laws need to be flexible enough to accommodate alternatives. There should be consideration for the plurality of legal opinions. However, the consistency provided by law in definitions and methods appears to have provided greater continuity and enhances enforceability in companies such as Sudan, where shari'ah legal positions are highly homogenous, and zakat is obligatory. When zakat is voluntary, the zakat assessment is more realistic than the results of a consultation between the muzakki (zakat payer) and the zakat collecting institutions.

vii. Competition however also means that teams would have an equal footing. Where the public body also takes on the function of the zakat regulator, it must limit it to supervision only, leaving the collection of zakat to private agencies. The entire zakat administration mechanism could also, through its own decentralized network, be undertaken by the public agency. The presence of private actors as agents of the public body is not prohibited in this type of situation, as is the case in Malaysian states.

Chapter 6 Zakat in Poverty Reduction

Introduction

Poverty is a dynamic and multifaceted problem that will continue to plague us in the near future. Countries have taken various steps to tackle poverty. However, one can demonstrate how the Islamic Zakat scheme, which is based on the holy Quran and Hadiths as well as proper marketing, can be used across the social spectrum to minimize poverty. Zakat can be seen as an alternative solution to poverty alleviation and capacity building for the vulnerable to become more active and contribute more to the economy.

Shirazi (2014) emphasizes the importance of zakat in reducing poverty. Zakat will cover up to 21% of Bangladesh's Annual Development Plan (ADP), which frees up other resources for social and development purposes. The overall effect of zakat is to increase demand, supply, and productivity, thus raising the government's ability to tax. Due to both the government and the IMF/World

Bank not recognizing the need to use zakat for poverty reduction, zakat is not employed as a tool for reducing poverty. Many Muslims, especially in Arab countries, have a reputation for donating their zakat, or charity, to the poor and various charities on their own. All of these transactions, on the other hand, are not going through the proper channels, are unrecorded, unplanned, and unrelated to any strategy. As a result, it is impossible to assess the efficacy of zakat in reducing poverty.

Zakat is one of Islam's five pillars. Zakat is an effective tool for achieving social justice. In Bangladesh, however, the majority of wealthy Muslims are unaware of the problem and are hesitant to pay zakat in a timely manner. It is limited to handing out saris and lungis to the needy, as well as a few dollars, without taking into account company profits and properties, liquid funds or investments, or a gold or silver reserve at the basic rate of 2.5 percent. Because of a lack of proper Islamic awareness among the Muslim population and because the mechanism has not been institutionalized publicly and privately, the collection and distribution of zakat funds has yet to be successful. Zakat helps to alleviate poverty and facilitates a more equal distribution of income.

For a long time, poverty has been a big problem and a significant obstacle in developing countries (Shirazi, 2014 and Badrudin & Siregar, 2015). Developing Bangladesh has similar problems. In contrast to the Muslim-majority Bangladesh, however, a zakat system developed in that country has the potential to help alleviate poverty and increase prosperity. The Islamic zakat scheme, on the other hand, has the same goal: to help the poor and alleviate poverty in a region. There is no interest added to the zakat number, and the beneficiaries are not expected to repay it. Zakat seeks to enrich the needy rather than only provide them with a means of subsistence. It functions as a social charitable giving tool, and if properly managed, the beneficiaries may set up small businesses to manufacture goods and meet their basic needs.

However, as with any poverty alleviation strategy, the poor's capacity should be built through health, education, and vocational training services, among other things, so that the poor can escape the poverty trap. Furthermore, the development of business entrepreneurship should be prioritized. Since entrepreneurship development programs will allow not only the abolition of poverty but also the creation of job opportunities for a large number of the poor.

The payment of zakah in the proper sum and system for alleviating poverty in Muslim society would eventually contribute to the Muslim world's stability, harmony, and prosperity. (Hoque et al. 2015)

Narrated by 'Adi bin Hatim:

"While I was sitting with Allah's Messenger (PBUH) two person came to him; one of them complained about his poverty and the other complained about the prevalence of robberies. Allah's Messenger (PBUH) said, "As regards stealing and robberies, there will shortly come a time when a caravan will go to Mecca (from Medina) without any guard. And regarding poverty, The Hour (Day of Judgment) will not be established till one of you wanders about with his object of charity and will not find anybody to accept it And (no doubt) each one of you will stand in front of Allah and there will be neither a curtain nor an interpreter between him and Allah, and Allah will ask him, 'Did not I give you wealth?' He will reply in the affirmative. Allah will further ask, 'Didn't send a messenger to you?' And again that person will reply in the affirmative Then he will look to his right and he will see nothing but Hell-fire, and then he will look to his left and will see nothing but Hell-fire. And so, any (each one) of you should save himself from the fire even by giving half of a date-fruit (in charity). And if you do not find a hall date fruit, then (you can do it through saying) a good pleasant word (to your brethren)." (Sahih al-Bukhari, Hadith No. 793 Vol. 4).

Narrated by Abu Mas`ud:

"When the verses of charity were revealed, we used to work as porters. A man came and distributed objects of charity in abundance. And they (the people) said, "He is showing off." And another man came and gave a Sa (a small measure of food grains); they said, "Allah is not in need of this small amount of charity." And then the Divine Inspiration came: "Those who criticize such of the believers who give in charity voluntarily and those who could not find to give in charity except what is available to them." (Quran 9:79), (Sahih al-Bukhari, 1415).

Narrated by Abu Mas`ud Al-Ansari:

"Whenever Allah's Messenger (PBUH) ordered us to give in charity, we used to go to the market and work as porters and get a Mudd (a special measure of grain) and then give it in charity. (Those were the days of poverty) and today some of us have one hundred thousand." (Sahih al-Bukhari, 1415)

Narrated by Abu Musa:

"Thy Prophet (ﷺ) said, "A time will come upon the people when a person will wander about with gold as Zakat and will not find anybody to accept it, and one man will be seen followed by forty women to be their guardian because of scarcity of men and great number of women."(Sahih al-Bukhari. 1414)

Many governments, including a number of Islamic ones, have found zakat to be an extremely effective economic tool for correcting the social shortcomings and ensuring fair compensation for the poor. Zakat also figured prominently in early Muslim history (Nadzri et al., 2012). Giving alms according to the zakat cleanses the soul from selfishness and greed and reduces the recipient's poverty. However, since the zakat (religious alms) gets paid, it in money, the money's use tends to multiply, which results in more people having access to wealth.

Poverty is a classic problem that has plagued humanity since the dawn of time. Poverty is a complicated topic that will presumably continue to be a concern from time to time. Many ways were utilized to help population mitigate poverty, including building better roads to make getting around, and providing access to transportation, facilitating small-scale market exchanges, and providing work opportunities for those who reside in rural areas, as well as building up governments that empower people to market their agricultural products.

While poverty is often interpreted as a lack of well-being, it does not have to be that way. Poverty is brought on by the way an economy, a political system, and a social structure are all interconnected those systems communicate with each other, thus producing social immobility among a group of individuals (World Bank 2000). The poor are highly susceptible to stress and unstable in a variety of ways. The fact that the vicious cycle of poverty seems to continue unabated is among the poor is one of the hallmarks of poverty (Basu 1984). Though poverty has gone from having to something much broader concepts such as exposure to risk, vulnerability, and voicelessness.

Even if a country is different from others, poverty is a global issue (Khan, 2001). There are nearly seven billion people on Earth, and nearly 40 percent of them are living in extreme poverty, which is described as less than $2 a day (Todaro and Smith, 2012). Even though poverty is worldwide, approximately 44% of the 1.7 billion people who reside in Muslim-majority nations (MMNs) reside in poverty (The Nation, 2013).

Mohsin(2013) recently reported two-digit poor rates in nine MMNs, including Pakistan (24%), Afghanistan (53%), Indonesia (18%), Iran (18%), Bangladesh (45%), Sudan (40%), Yemen (45%), Algeria (23%), Egypt (20%) and Nigeria (70 per cent). A total of 335 million people are in poverty in the countries listed above. Inadequate governance policies trigger great income inequality, which contributes to the MNN problem (Carvalho, 2009). Some other causes of poverty in developing countries include the stigma that comes from being born in poverty, the harshness of the environment, gender issues, market barriers, and counterproductive public policies (Khan, 2001). Since the beginning of the 1960s, governments, scholars, and international organizations have been concerned about fighting poverty (United Nations, 2000; Todaro and Smith, 2012; Raimi and Mobolaji, 2008). policies that address reducing income inequality and increasing food security can both be considered to be poverty reduction measures (Ravallion, 2005). In addition, governments provide poor people with basic commodities so that they spend 80% of their income on food (Barrette and Beardmore, 2000). Strategies that address the root causes of poverty and social change are most effective in disadvantaged communities where inclusion, caste systems, and socioeconomic disparity are widespread (Kar, 2007; Rao, 2010).

The mainstream Islamic clerics and economists have recommended that using Zakat, Waqf, and interest-free loans known as Qard Hasan in contemporary Muslim societies would result in social justice, equity, and income redistribution (Cizakca, 2004; Ahmed, 2007). Zakat is a necessary alms, which ensures that the poor receive 2.5% of a person's net wealth per year (Doi, 1990; Adebayo, 2008). As an obligatory requirement, the minimum taxable sum known as "nisab" should be paid on at least 14 wealth products and the properties of individuals (Mohsin, 2013).

It is impossible to solve poverty because it is a complex, multi-dimensional experience that affects not only the poor but also whole communities and their economies (Fukuda-Parr, 2006, p. 7). Furthermore, poverty is a "responsibility for poverty," which is prevalent in numerous societies because of a variety of other contributing factors, including "political, economic, social, and cultural influences" (Carney, 1992, p. 74). The term "poverty" describes the depravity that is created by the money that other people earn. According to Chambers (2006), poverty can be described as the lack of income and content, along with physical capacity and a wide range of human needs.

Macro Dimensions of Poverty

Romer (1986) and Lucas (1988) stressed the importance of human capital in the development process instead of the capitalist accumulation process. A large scale of investment in human resources provides externalities and productivity benefits. The corollary to this assumption is that intelligence is considered to be comprised of both physical resources and labor input. If the body of information grows, human and physical resources increases, productivity, boosting the overall economy's ability to generate both physical and profits. In this viewpoint, it is believed that countries and peoples are impoverished because of resources, rather than having less money (World Bank 1999). Where there is growth in the gross national income, there will be growth in average income, but which community takes home the growth will influence overall poverty levels is a matter of who gets the benefit. Poverty can only be eradicated through distribution of the country's income.

However, economic growth may affect distribution and poverty levels of resources between sectors and population groups. The relationship between growth and inequality was studied at earlier papers by Kuznets (1954) and Lewis (1954). The theories for the first phase of development forecast the growth of income inequality. After reaching a threshold amount of percapita revenue, economic growth leads to more balanced distribution of income. But there is no systematic connection between growth and inequity in empirical studies (Ferreira 1999, Dollar and Kraay 2002). Some research suggests that rapid development has not led to further disparity, however, studies contend that equality of opportunity has served to exacerbate already existing inequity. Differential development, in some way, will have an effect on poverty.

Poverty in the Islamic Worldview

Islam, as a philosophy of balance, places equal focus on spiritual and worldly matters. In addition, poverty represents both the absence of things to be desired and the presence of things that are not provided. There is no indicator of human well-being at all for the Muslim. This is because it is impossible to put a monetary value on the spiritual element. A Muslim's health is made up of both the physical and the spiritual. However, we cannot extend the same logic to society. It is because our well-being is not primarily concerned with spirituality. God does not judge the community, but man is presented before God as individuals in the Hereafter. The Islamic view is that poverty is an issue with the system, because Allah has made provisions for everyone to be sustained in life.

Allah (SWT) said in Qur'an,

اَللهُ الَّذِىْ خَلَقَكُمْ ثُمَّ رَزَقَكُمْ ثُمَّ يُمِيْتُكُمْ ثُمَّ يُحْيِيْكُمْ ۖ هَلْ مِنْ شُرَكَآئِكُمْ مَّنْ يَّفْعَلُ مِنْ ذٰ لِكُمْ مِّنْ شَىْءٍ سُبْحٰنَهٗ وَتَعٰلٰى عَمَّا يُشْرِكُوْنَ

"So, set you your face towards the religion as a Hanif. Allah's Fitrah with which He has created mankind. No change let there be in Allah's Khalq, that is the straight religion, but most men know not." (Qur'an, 30:40)

وَمَا مِنْ دَآ بَّةٍ فِى الْأَرْضِ إِلَّا عَلَى اللهِ رِزْقُهَا وَ يَعْلَمُ مُسْتَقَرَّهَا وَمُسْتَوْدَعَهَا كُلٌّ فِىْ كِتٰبٍ مُّبِيْنٍ

"And no moving creature is there on earth but its provision is due from Allah. And He knows its dwelling place and its deposit. All is in a Clear Book." (Qur'an, 11:6)

هُوَ الَّذِىْ جَعَلَ لَكُمُ الْأَرْضَ ذَلُوْلًا فَامْشُوْا فِىْ مَنَاكِبِهَا وَكُلُوْا مِنْ رِزْقِهٖ وَإِلَيْهِ النُّشُوْرُ

"At the same time Islam has closed the opportunity for cultural poverty by giving the obligation for every individual to seeking earning life. "He is Who has made the earth subservient to you; so walk in the paths thereof and eat of His

provision. And to Him will be the resurrection." (Qur'an, 67 :15)

فَإِذَا قُضِيَتِ الصَّلٰوةُ فَانْتَشِرُوْا فِى الْأَرْضِ وَابْتَغُوْا مِنْ فَضْلِ اللهِ وَاذْكُرُوا اللهَ كَثِيْرًا لَّعَلَّكُمْ تُفْلِحُوْنَ

"And does not restrict the human to seek provision unless under sharia rules.
*"Then when the Salah is complete, you may disperse through the land, and seek
the bounty of Allah, and remember Allah much, that you may be successful."
(Qur'an, 62 : 10)*

Even Islam encourages human to seek provision considering as part of the
Allah's worship,

لَيْسَ الْبِرَّ أَنْ تُوَلُّوا وُجُوْهَكُمْ قِبَلَ الْمَشْرِقِ وَ الْمَغْرِبِ وَلٰكِنَّ الْبِرَّ مَنْ أَمَنَ بِاللهِ وَالْيَوْمِ الْأَخِرِ
وَالْمَلٰئِكَةِ وَالْكِتٰبِ وَالنَّبِيّٖنَ وَأَتَى الْمَالَ عَلٰى حُبِّهٖ ذَوِى الْقُرْبٰى وَالْيَتٰمٰى وَالْمَسٰكِيْنَ وَابْنَ السَّبِيْلِ
وَالسَّائِلِيْنَ وَفِى الرِّقَابِ وَأَقَامَ الصَّلٰوةَ وَأَتَى الزَّكٰوةَ وَالْمُوْفُوْنَ بِعَهْدِهِمْ إِذَا عٰهَدُوْا وَالصّٰبِرِيْنَ
فِى الْبَأْسَاءِ وَالضَّرَّاءِ وَحِيْنَ الْبَأْسِ أُولٰئِكَ الَّذِيْنَ صَدَقُوْا وَأُولٰئِكَ هُمُ الْمُتَّقُوْنَ

*"It is not Birr that you turn your faces towards east and (or) west; but Birr is the
one who believes in Allah, the Last Day, the Angels, the Book, the Prophets and
gives his wealth, in spite of love for it, to the kinsfolk, to the orphans, and to Al-
Masakin (the poor), and to the wayfarer, and to those who ask, and to set
servants free, performs As Salah (Iqamat-As-Salah), and gives the Zakah, and
who fulfill their covenant when they make it, and who are patient in extreme
poverty and ailment (disease) and at the time of fighting (during the battles).
Such are the people of the truth and they are Al-Muttaqun (the pious)." (Qur'an,
2 : 177)*

وَمَا خَلَقْتُ الْجِنَّ وَالْإِنْسَ إِلَّا لِيَعْبُدُوْنِ

*"And I created not the Jinn and mankind except that they should worship Me."
(Qur'an, 51 : 56)*

وَكَأَيِّنْ مِّنْ دَابَّةٍ لَّا تَحْمِلُ رِزْقَهَا اللهُ يَرْزُقُهَا وَإِيَّاكُمْ وَهُوَ السَّمِيْعُ الْعَلِيْمُ

Each creature has sustenance, so they will not starve, *"And so many a moving creatures carries not its provision! Allah provides for it and for you. And He is the All-Hearer, the All- Knower." (Qur'an 29 : 60)*

"You will never be hungry therein nor naked. "And you (will) suffer not from thirst therein nor from the sun's heat." (Qur'an, 118-119)

Because provision is Allah's prerogative,

فَإِذَا بَلَغْنَ أَجَلَهُنَّ فَأَمْسِكُوْهُنَّ بِمَعْرُوْفٍ أَوْ فَارِقُوْهُنَّ بِمَعْرُوْفٍ وَّأَشْهِدُوْا ذَوَىْ عَدْلٍ مِّنْكُمْ وَأَقِيْمُوا الشَّهَادَةَ لِلهِ ۚ ذٰ لِكُمْ يُوْعَظُ بِهٖ مَنْ كَانَ يُؤْمِنُ بِاللهِ وَالْيَوْمِ الْأخِرِ ۚ وَمَنْ يَّتَّقِ اللهَ يَجْعَلْ لَّهٗ مَخْرَجًا ۚ

وَّيَرْزُقْهُ مِنْ حَيْثُ لَا يَحْتَسِبُ ۚ وَمَنْ يَّتَوَكَّلْ عَلَى اللهِ فَهُوَ حَسْبُهٗ ۚ إِنَّ اللهَ بَالِغُ أَمْرِهٖ ۚ قَدْ جَعَلَ اللهُ لِكُلِّ شَىْءٍ قَدْرًا

"Then, when they are about to attain their term appointed, either taking them back in a good manner or part with them in a good manner. And take as witness two just persons from among you. And establish the testimony for Allah. That will be an admonition given to him who believes in Allah and the Last Day. And whosoever has Taqwa of Allah, He will make a way for him to get out.) (3. And He will provide him from where he never could imagine. And whosoever puts his trust in Allah, and then He will suffice him. Verily, Allah will accomplish his purpose. Indeed Allah has set a measure for all things." (Qur'an, 65:2-3)

وَمَا مِنْ دَآ بَّةٍ فِى الْأَرْضِ إِلَّا عَلَى اللهِ رِزْقُهَا وَ يَعْلَمُ مُسْتَقَرَّهَا وَمُسْتَوْدَعَهَا كُلٌّ فِىْ كِتٰبٍ مُّبِيْنٍ

"And has guaranteed the provision for every creature in exactly size of each, "And no moving creature is there on earth but its provision is due from Allah. And He knows its dwelling place and its deposit. All is in a Clear Book." (Qur'an, 11 : 6)

So Islam actually encourages people to not fear to the poverty and lack of economic resources:

قُلْ تَعَالَوْا أَتْلُ مَا حَرَّمَ رَبُّكُمْ عَلَيْكُمْ أَلَّا تُشْرِكُوا بِهِ شَيْئًا وَّبِالْوَالِدَيْنِ إِحْسَانًا ۖ وَلَا تَقْتُلُوٓا أَوْلَادَكُم مِّنْ إِمْلَاقٍ نَّحْنُ نَرْزُقُكُمْ وَإِيَّاهُمْ ۖ وَلَا تَقْرَبُوا الْفَوَاحِشَ مَا ظَهَرَ مِنْهَا وَمَا بَطَنَ ۖ وَلَا تَقْتُلُوا النَّفْسَ الَّتِي حَرَّمَ اللَّهُ إِلَّا بِالْحَقِّ ۚ ذَٰلِكُمْ وَصَّىٰكُم بِهِ لَعَلَّكُمْ تَعْقِلُونَ

"Say: "Come, I will recite what your Lord has prohibited you from: Join not anything in worship with Him; be kind and dutiful to your parents; kill not your children because of poverty -- We provide sustenance for you and for them. Come not near to Al-Fawahish (immoral sins) whether committed openly or secretly; and kill not anyone whom Allah has forbidden, except for a just cause. This He has commanded you that you may understand." (Qur'an, 6 : 151)

In the Islamic perspective, poverty is caused by various structural reasons. First, poverty arise because wickedness of man against nature,

ظَهَرَ الْفَسَادُ فِى الْبَرِّ وَالْبَحْرِ بِمَا كَسَبَتْ أَيْدِى النَّاسِ لِيُذِيْقَهُمْ بَعْضَ الَّذِىْ عَمِلُوْا لَعَلَّهُمْ يَرْجِعُوْنَ

"Evil has appeared in Al-Barr and Al-Bahr because of what the hands of men have earned, that He may make them taste a part of that which they have done, in order that they may return." (Qur'an, 30:41)

So the human himself who feel the impact of his wickedness,

وَمَآ أَصَابَكُمْ مِّنْ مُّصِيْبَةٍ فَبِمَا كَسَبَتْ أَيْدِيْكُمْ وَيَعْفُوْا عَنْ كَثِيْرٍ

"And whatever of misfortune befalls you, it is because of what your hands have earned. And He pardons much. And you cannot escape from Allah in the earth, and besides Allah you have neither any protector nor any helper." (Qur'an :42 :30)

Second, poverty arises because ignorance and stinginess from rich group,

وَلَا يَحْسَبَنَّ الَّذِيْنَ يَبْخَلُوْنَ بِمَآ اٰتٰهُمُ اللهُ مِنْ فَضْلِهٖ هُوَ خَيْرًا لَّهُمْ بَلْ هُوَ شَرٌّ لَّهُمْ سَيُطَوَّقُوْنَ مَا بَخِلُوْا بِهٖ يَوْمَ الْقِيٰمَةِ ۗ وَ لِلّٰهِ مِيْرَاثُ السَّمٰوٰتِ وَالْأَرْضِ ۗ وَاللهُ بِمَا تَعْمَلُوْنَ خَبِيْرٌ

"And let not those who are stingy with that which Allah has bestowed on them of His bounty think that it is good for them. Nay, it will be worse for them; the things that they were stingy with shall be tied to their necks like a collar on the Day of Resurrection. And Allah's is the inheritance of the heavens and the earth; and Allah is Well-Acquainted with all that you do." (Qur'an, 3 : 180)

وَجَمَعَ فَأَوْعٰى

"And collect (wealth) and hide it (from spending it in the cause of Allah." (Qur'an, 70 : 18)

So that the poor people are not able to exit from poverty. Third, poverty arises because some people are being arbitrary, exploitative, and oppressive to some other man, like eating someone else's property by way of vanity,

وَلَا تَبْخَسُوا النَّاسَ أَشْيَآءَهُمْ وَلَا تَعْثَوْا فِى الْأَرْضِ مُفْسِدِيْنَ

"And defraud not people by reducing their things, nor do evil, making corruption and mischief in the land." (Qur'an, 26:183)

وَلَا تَدْعُ مَعَ اللهِ إِلٰهًا اٰخَرَ ۘ لَا إِلٰهَ إِلَّا هُوَ ۚ كُلُّ شَىْءٍ هَالِكٌ إِلَّا وَجْهَهٗ ۚ لَهُ الْحُكْمُ وَإِلَيْهِ تُرْجَعُوْنَ

"O you who believe! Verily, there are many of the Ahbar (rabbis) and the Ruhban (monks) who devour the wealth of mankind in falsehood, and hinder (them) from the way of Allah. And those who hoard up gold and silver and spend them not in the way of Allah, announce unto them a painful torment." (Quran, 28:88)

Fourth, poverty arises because the concentration of political power, bureaucracy, and economy in one hand. This is illustrated in the story of Pharaoh, Haman, and Korah are allied in oppressing the people of Egypt in the life of Prophet Musa.

In such, in Islam justice and equality has been always as an important instrument in fighting poverty:

يَـٰٓأَيُّهَا الَّذِينَ أَمَنُوا كُوْنُوا قَوَّا امِينَ لِلَّهِ شُهَدَاءَ بِالْقِسْطِ ۖ وَلَا يَجْرِمَنَّكُمْ شَنَأَنُ قَوْمٍ عَلَى اَ لَّا تَعْدِلُوا ۚ اِعْدِلُوا هُوَ اَقْرَبُ لِلتَّقْوَى وَاتَّقُوا اللَّهَ ۚ إِنَّ اللَّهَ خَبِيْرٌ بِمَا تَعْمَلُوْنَ

"O you who believe! Stand out firmly for Allah as just witnesses; and let not the enmity and hatred of others make you avoid justice. Be just, that is nearer to Taqwa; and have Taqwa of Allah. Verily, Allah is Well-Acquainted with what you do." (Qur'an, 5:8)

Fifth, the poverty caused by external shocks such as natural disasters or wars, so the land which was originally rich turned into a poor. Natural disasters such as that struck this impoverish the people of Saba,

فَلَمَّا قَضَيْنَا عَلَيْهِ الْمَوْتَ مَا دَلَّهُمْ عَلَى مَوْتِهِ إِلَّا دَآ بَّةُ الْأَرْضِ تَأْ كُلُ مِنْسَأَتَهُ ۖ فَلَمَّا خَرَّ تَبَيَّنَتِ الْجِنُّ اَنْ لَّوْ كَانُوا يَعْلَمُوْنَ الْغَيْبَ مَا لَبِثُوا فِى الْعَذَابِ الْمُهِيْنِ ۛ

لَقَدْ كَانَ لِسَبَإٍ فِىْ مَسْكَنِهِمْ أَيَةٌ ۖ جَنَّتْنِ عَنْ يَّمِيْنٍ وَّشِمَالٍ ۖ كُلُوا مِنْ رِّزْقِ رَبِّكُمْ وَاشْكُرُوْا لَهُ ۚ بَلْدَةٌ طَيِّبَةٌ وَّرَبٌّ غَفُوْرٌ

"Then when We decreed death for him, nothing informed them (Jinn) of his death except a little worm of the earth which kept (slowly) gnawing away at his stick. So when he fell down, the Jinn saw clearly that if they had known the Unseen, they would not have stayed in the humiliating torment Indeed there was for Saba' a sign in their dwelling place -- two gardens on the right and on the left; (and it was said to them), "Eat the provision of your Lord, and be grateful to Him." A fair land and an Oft Forgiving Lord." (Qur'an, 34;14-15)

or the wars that created the poor refugees who were expelled from his country. And there is also a share in this booty for the poor emigrants, who were expelled from their homes and their property, seeking bounties from Allah and (His) good pleasure, and helping Allah and His Messenger (PBUH). Such are indeed the truthful.

لِلْفُقَرَاءِ الْمُهٰجِرِيْنَ الَّذِيْنَ أُخْرِجُوْا مِنْ دِيَارِهِمْ وَأَمْوَالِهِمْ يَبْتَغُوْنَ فَضْلًا مِّنَ اللهِ وَرِضْوَانًا وَّيَنْصُرُوْنَ اللهَ وَرَسُوْلَهٗ أُولٰٓئِكَ هُمُ الصّٰدِقُوْنَ

وَالَّذِيْنَ تَبَوَّؤُ الدَّارَ وَالْإِيْمَانَ مِنْ قَبْلِهِمْ يُحِبُّوْنَ مَنْ هَاجَرَ اِلَيْهِمْ وَلَا يَجِدُوْنَ فِىْ صُدُوْرِهِمْ حَاجَةً مِّمَّا أُوْتُوْا وَيُؤْثِرُوْنَ عَلٰى اَنْفُسِهِمْ وَلَوْ كَانَ بِهِمْ خَصَاصَةٌ ۚ وَمَنْ يُّوْقَ شُحَّ نَفْسِهٖ فَأُولٰٓئِكَ هُمُ الْمُفْلِحُوْنَ

"And (it is also for) those who, before them, had homes and had adopted the faith, love those who emigrate to them, and have no jealousy in their breasts for that which they have been given, and give them preference over themselves even though they were in need of that. And whosoever is saved from his greed, such are they who will be the successful). And those who came after them say: "Our Lord! Forgive us and our brethren who have preceded us in faith, and put not in our hearts any hatred against those who have believed. Our Lord! You are indeed full of kindness, Most Merciful." (Qur'an, 59:8-9)

Chapter 7

Zakat for Empowerment

Introduction

The process of facilitating and nurturing the poor is called empowerment. Disadvantaged people's empowerment is usually consistent with ideas of justice, democracy, commitment and networking in the theory of community growth (Soetomo, 2015). Person and social strength and engagement is an essential component in the development of democracy and empowerment (Pramanik, 1998: 19). The participation of zakat institutions in this case is intended for the poor, rather than creating lifelong dependence, in building self trust and the ability to stand alone. The effort is made together to allow the poor to dedicate more time to their lives to gain trust, self-esteem and experience to acquire new skills. The procedure is done in steps, so that the better an individual will participate (Riyadi, 2014). At the core stage, economic empowerment in the communities is an effort to offer people the education, skills and self-confidence to develop a better socio-economic life. In short, the goal of social economic empowerment is to create people who depend on socio-economic self-sufficiency.

The aim of the zakat effort is to motivate mustahiq to develop a spirit of entrepreneurship (social entrepreneurship) to help them earn a good living while helping the community around them. Creation of Mustahiq's skills in the field of schooling, coaching, and training and by providing companies with Zakat capital credits aims to empower them. One of the main objectives of zakat distribution is to give the poor (Mustahiq) the resources they need to be able to afford necessities and sustain themselves and their families. The freedom of Mustahiq is vital to overcome social inequality, exclusion, unemployment and poverty. This can only be done by using zakat as a tool to motivate people economically, to increase their ability and to develop into entrepreneurs so that they can meet their own needs.

Zakat is one of the Islamic economic instruments used to alleviate social inequity by empowering the poor. Assets created by wealthy community organizations are used to economically empower vulnerable groups, enabling them to grow and improve their well-being. Mustahiq's financial independence is crucial in resolving the community's inequality issue, which stifles long-term development. Inequality of welfare in a society's social structure can lead to the growth of a number of social problems, such as crime and poverty, affecting the community's overall quality of life. In this case, Zakat seeks to tackle the root cause of poverty, namely the lack of efforts and activity of citizens. Poverty can be mitigated by zakat by assisting the poor to meet their basic needs instead of helping the poor to break the cycle of poverty.

The Zakat obligation is not just a way of shifting money from the rich to the poor. Zakat must also serve as a tool for economic growth, having repercussions for the welfare of the population, including growing lower-class economic efficiency, increased overall use, increased overall investment and, therefore, increased employment. In other words, zakat must also become a tool to motivate the poor to be free of poverty and ultimately become muzakki (Economic empowerment).

Zakat seeks to enhance the capacity of the poor by enhancing the elements of empowerment, enabling them to raise their quality of life and living by means of their own efforts. The hope is that they are able to break free of poverty and backwardness by instilling a sense of dignity and self-confidence in the poor. With the participation of productive zakat, a balance is achieved in the distribution of land, not only through a redistribution of assets, but also through the redistribution of funds and through the provision of services and skills in order to break the cycle of poverty (Nurzaman, 2016). This active zakat is very useful to poor people who want to start a business or already have one, but are unable to grow because of a lack of money (Kasri, 2016).

Zakat and Youth Empowerment

Zakat is an Islamic social finance instrument that has a significant effect on a country's socioeconomic growth. Unemployment, from an Islamic viewpoint, is a state in which an individual refuses to use his or her physical and spiritual abilities to achieve a gain that is approved by Sharia. Person factors and the socioeconomic system are also factors that contribute to unemployment. Individual characteristics such as laziness, disability, and a lack of knowledge and skills are all contributing factors. While socioeconomic factors such as limited job opportunities, the dominance of non-real economic sectors, and other factors all play a role (Syamsuri, 2018).

Zakat, also known as Islamic philanthropy, is one of Islam's five pillars and has a significant effect on personal, social, and economic dimensions. Zakat can be seen as one of the methods for inspiring young people who are unemployed. The zakat institutions' youth empowerment program is in line with one of the Sustainable Development Goals (SDGs) number 8, which is Decent Work and Economic Growth. Maqashid Sharia is located in the wealth dimension (hifdzul maal) and meets Dharuriyah requirements.

The effectiveness of the mustahik empowerment program is expected to lead to the individual and social well-being of mustahik people. According to Zaenal et al. (2018), economic empowerment by zakat has a major effect on poverty reduction and inequality reduction. Furthermore, according to Pailis et al. (2016), the empowerment of mustahik would have an effect on both individual and community welfare.

According to Jennings et al. (2006), empowerment is a social action mechanism that can take place at different levels, including individuals, families, organisations, and communities. Empowerment in zakat institutions is typically used to maximize the use of efficient zakat by providing unique business resources and a companion function to help mustahik companies become more self-sufficient. As a result, the empowerment program has a long-term, sustainable, and positive character (Sahroni et al, 2019).

Youth empowerment can be described as a series of coordinated activities aimed at instilling trust in young people by providing inspiration and access to information and skills based on their interests and potential. According to Tope (2011), the process of youth empowerment focuses on an individual's mindset, structural, and cultural aspects through which he gains the capacity, authority, and agency to make decisions and enact changes in his own life (Gill et al., 2018).

According to the findings of Mohajer and Earnest's research (2009), one of the factors to consider in a youth empowerment program is skill growth. According to Lakin & Mahoney (2006), the components of a youth empowerment program are divided into three phases: capacity development, preparation, and intervention. Organizational support, according to Roadess & Eisenberger (2002), can take the form of policies, norms, community, law, morality, and finances. Other factors that affect empowerment, according to Baird & Wang (2008), include organizational factors that will aid in the preparation of the empowerment program to include the expertise and skills they need. Community empowerment projects that succeed would undoubtedly provide insight about how to live a healthier life (Conger & Kanungo, 1988). External factors such as service providers, knowledge providers, capital providers, and marketing of business results are all examples of institutional support, according to Hamzah (2017).

Meanwhile, research conducted by Muhamat et al. (2013) shows that zakat institutions' resources and expertise have a positive impact and connection on Asnaf's business performance in Malaysia. Afzali et al. (2014) found that organizational support has an important impact on empowerment based on the findings of other empirical studies.

As one of the instruments of Islamic social finance that is controlled and optimized by zakat institutions, zakat plays an important role in youth empowerment programs. Zakat institutions promote youth development programs by providing facilities and resources, as well as information about skills, leadership, entrepreneurship, and religious understanding, as well as providing business capital assistance and forming alliances with businesses. Thus, the relationship between zakat institution support and individual welfare was completely mediated by the success of the youth empowerment program.

Zakat's Role in Empowering the Poor

A big portion of the zakat usage program is something needed in order to have long-term benefits of zakat and to boost the socio-economic worth of zakat money, one of which is the community's social empowerment program.

It is vital to develop several techniques of zakat-based social empowerment that are successful in reducing low empowerment performance and increasing the social value of zakat (Tampubolon et al., 2006).

Darwanto (2010) said the definition of increased freedom of choice and action refers to empowerment. This freedom is severely limited to a poor society because of its voicelessness and impotence with government and market relevance. The empowerment of the poor and retarded societies requires efforts to remove the reasons for impotence to improve the quality of their lives. Empowerment is both a process and an outcome according to Luttrell et al. (2009). Empowerment is an endeavour to empower the underprivileged society.

Zakat is one of Islam's five pillars. It is a wealth redistribution mechanism in which Muslims who earn more than a particular amount must donate their income to the most vulnerable populations, including the impoverished and needy. These contributions can be used to deal with gender inequalities when appropriately channeled and with systematic planning.

According to a recent study conducted by UNDP and the Center for Economics and Development Studies at the University of Padjajaran using the donation channel Rumah Zakat, the majority of households benefiting from women's entrepreneurship funding programs are also the beneficiaries of government social protection programs.

Women entrepreneurs can use zakat cash to launch their firm with funding from government social protection programs as capital to support business operations. In accordance with the Sustainable Development Goals (SDGs) Program for Gender Equality and Women, the zakat money distributed to women's micro and small enterprises. Zakat can give an alternate or a new way of delivering money to, or even complement, existing social protection programmes. Zakat funding could also give beneficiaries more access by moving their payments from a consumptive model to a productive model, which is targeted through a program of empowerment. In this way, zakat focuses on production such as the transfer of initial capital and training.

In order to raise public awareness of giving zakat to trusted organizations, developing partnerships between government and civilian society is essential. This allows the implementation and regular evaluation of non-cash assistance programs to support women's empowerment programs requiring huge sums of funding.

Zakat Community Development is a group empowerment program that integrates social aspects (education, health, advocacy, the environment, and other humanities) with comprehensive economic aspects, with the primary funding coming from zakat, donations, and alms in order to create a prosperous and self-sufficient society.

Shifting to Islamic financing is a sensible step. Islam is a religion that respects the concepts of justice and equality, with its Holy book stating that women and men should have equal access to economic possibilities.

Research results by Sartika (2008) reveal that the amount of funds distributed and the recipient earnings are significantly influenced. This means that the amount of zakat distributed really affects the income of the beneficiary. Beik's (2009) research suggests that zakat reduces the number of poor families from 84% to 74%.

Conclusion

The backbone of Islamic social finance is zakat. It comes from a heavenly source and has the capacity to improve social welfare in the Muslim community. Zakat is one of the Islamic economic mechanisms that tries to alleviate the problem of social inequity by empowering the poor. Assets earned by successful community organizations are used to economically empower vulnerable groups, allowing them to expand and improve their well-being.

Zakat's societal aim is to eliminate poverty and the want to accumulate people at all costs and foster a conduct that is socially oriented. Zakat attempts to reduce socio-economic gaps by supporting and offering financial assistance to those who do not want to bring them closer to the havens. Zakat is an effective annual means for redistributing money to ensure that the needy are properly managed and that full employment is achieved.

Sustainable health is one of the objectives of the distribution of zakat, which means that the poor (mustahiq) may survive not only by fulfilling basic necessities, they may work and satisfy their own wants and their families. The independence of Mustahiq is vital in solving the problem of social inequality, exclusion, unemployment and poverty. This can only be done if zakat can be used as a way to enhance the poor's economic potential and enable them to become entrepreneurs and therefore to meet their own needs.

Zakat is a core of Islam that has to be computed, paid and spent every year. However, some believe that zakat is an act owed to God, while others are an obligation towards man. There is between these two points of view a spiritually substantial bridge of the truth, known personally and easily by early generations of Muslims. The rich thank God for their excess and by which they cleanse their wealth. This is a worshiping act. But God's confidence in the wealthy who matures every year is also a faith; and divine justice compels them to give it to its righteous owners on its own terms: the poor and needy.

According to Islamic law, every area of life must be regulated by laws. Wealth in this world and salvation in the next go hand in hand. The fifth pillar of Islam is zakat, or charity tax. Besides its importance as a religious requirement, zakat also includes qualities pertaining to poverty reduction and economic growth. The belief is that Islam, one of the existing religions in the world, provides goodwill to the world. In the Islamic tradition, Zakat is a category that encompasses both ritualized worship (i.e. "ibadah") and charity (i.e. "muamalah"). Helping the correct receivers with zakat can increase both the wealth of the world and the virtue of the one who made the zakat payment. Under the zakat system, Islamic finance can help drive sustainable economic development, help the poor get a grip on their finances, and help the less fortunate gain access to financial services. The zakat system is complementary to government efforts of poverty alleviation since it conceptualizes poverty the same way the government does.

Islam advocates for the abolition of absolute poverty and the organization of economic life in such a way that all human beings' basic necessities are provided.

To ensure that everyone's fundamental requirements are met, Islam enunciates the notion of the poor having a "right" in the income and riches of the well-off members of society through the zakat system. Zakat is a one-of-a-kind method for transferring money and wealth from the haves to the have-nots in the community. Zakat ensures that every individual in society has a minimal means of subsistence, which serves as a social security system in an Islamic community. Throughout history, whenever Muslims faithfully utilized the zakat system as prescribed by Shariah, the commendable and glorious goals of zakat were met.

The point is that transforming a community into a zakat-conscious one is not a philosophical issue. It is a very purposeful, practical, and open campaign to change our inner attitudes as Muslims, both inside ourselves and amongst ourselves. We should encourage one another, exhort one another, and assist relatives and neighbors in becoming aware of zakat, being exact in its calculation, methodical in its payment, and thorough in its disbursement.

References

Abang Mohamad Shibli, (2002). Peranan Zakat Dalam Pembangunan Ummah, Dalam Nik Mustapha Nik Hassan, (2002). Ekonomi Islam dan Pelaksanaannya di Malaysia, Kuala Lumpur, IKIM.

Abdul Aziz Muhammad, (1993). Zakat and Rural Developement in Malaysia. Kuala Lumpur: Berita Publishing.

Abdul Monir Yaacob, (2001). Garis Panduan Agama Dalam Pengagihan Dana Zakat. Dalam Nik Mustapha Nik

Abdul, A, et al. (1995). Institutional Framework of Zakat: Dimensions and Implications, Islamic Development Bank, Jeddah, Saudia.

Abdus-Salam, M. (1976). The Role of Fiscal and Accounting Thought in applying Zakat, unpublished. Presented at First International Conference on Islamic Economics, Makka.

Abdullah Ibrahim (1999), 'Agihan zakat menurut prinsip siasah shariyyah', Proceedings of Kolokium Keberkesanan Zakat Negeri Selangor.

Ab Rahman, A. et.al (2012). Zakah Institutions in Malaysia: Problem and Issues, Global Journal Al-Thaqafah, 2 (1): 31-40.

Abu Bakar, Nur B. A. Rahman, and A. Rahim (2007) A Comparative Study of Zakat and Modern Taxation. Journal of King Abdul Aziz University: Islamic Economics 20:1, 25– 40.

Adebayo, R. I. (2011). Zakah and Poverty Alleviation: A lesson for the Fiscal Policy Makers in Nigeria. Journal of Islamic Economics, Banking and Finance, 7(4): 26-41.

Abu 'Ubaid, al Qasim bin Sallam (1353H) al Amwal (circa 224 H), al Matba'ah al Tijariyyah al Kubra Publishers, Cairo (in Arabic).

Afzal ur Rahman, (1974). Economic Doctrine of Islam. Jil 2. Lahore: Islamic Publication Ltd.

Afzalurrahman, (1991). Doktrin Ekonomi Islam. Jil. 2. Kuala Lumpur:DBP.

Ahmad 'Atiyatullah, (1970). Al-Qamus al-Islami, Mesir, al-Nahdah, Vol. III.

Ahmed. H (2004)."Role of Zakah and Awqaf in poverty alleviation". Islamic Development Bank, Islamic Research and training institute, Jeddah. Occasional Paper No. 8

Afzali, A., Motahari, A. A. & Hatami-Shirkauhi, L. (2014). Investigating the Influence of Perceived Organizational Support, Psycological empowerment and Organizational Learning on Job Performance : An Empirical Investigation. Technical Gazette, 21 (3).

Ahmad, A. (1981). Some Basic Issues of Fiscal Policy in Islamic Economy, paper resented for International Conference of Muslim Scholars, Islamabad.

Adebayo, M.B. (2008), "Zakat: the Neglected Pillar, Al-Maslaha", Journal of Law and Religion, Vol. 4 No. 1, pp. 144-156.

Ahmed, H. (2007), "Waqf-based microfinance: realizing the social role of Islamic finance", presentation at International Seminar on Integrating Awqaf in the Islamic Financial Sector, Singapore, 6-7 March.

Ahmad, M.A.I. (2001), "Poverty alleviation and the third world", Pakistan Economic and Social Review, Vol. XXXIX No. 1, pp. 49-56.

AAOIFI (2008), Financial Accounting Standards, Accounting and Auditing Organization for Islamic Financial Institutions, Manama, Bahrain.

AAOIFI (2010), Financial Accounting Standards, Accounting and Auditing Organization for Islamic Financial Institutions. Manama, Bahrain.

Al-'Ayni, (1972). 'Umdah al-Qari' Sharh Sahih al-Bukhari, Mesir, Mustafa al-Halabi, Vol.VII.

Al Ghazali, Abi Hamid Muhammad bin Muhammad al Ghazali,. n.d. Al Mustasfa min 'Ilmi al Usul. Beirut.

Ali, I., & Hatta, Z. A. (2014). Zakat as a poverty reduction mechanism among the Muslim community: Case study of Bangladesh, Malaysia, and Indonesia. Asian Social Work and Policy Review, 8(1), 59–70.

Ali, M. G. (1963). Zakat wa Sadaqat ka Nizam (The System of Zakat and Sadaqat) (Urdu), Tarjumnaul-Quran, 60 (2), 114-17.

Al-Qardawi, Y. (1999). Fiqh Az-Zakat: A Comparative Study, Dar Al Taqwa, Ltd. London, UK

Al-Qaradhawi, Y. (2000). Fiqh Al Zakah: A Comparative Study of Zakah, Regulations and Philosophy in the Light of Quran and Sunnah. Saudi Arabia: King Abdul Aziz University.

Al Qaradawi, Yusuf (1973), Fiqh al Zakah, Mu'assasat al Risalah Publishers, 2nd printing Beirut (in Arabic).

Al Qarhawi, (1987). Fiqh al Zakat. Beirut: Muassasah al Risalah.

Al Syatibi, Abi Ishak. n.d. Al Muwafaqat fi Usul al Syariah. Beirut.

Ataina Hudayati & Achmad Tohirin (2010), 'Management of zakah: centralized vs decentralized approach', Proceedings of Seventh International Conference – The Tawhidi Epistemology: Zakat and Waqf Economy

Awad, Mohamed H. (1989). Adjusting Tax Structure to Accommodate Zakah. In I.M.

Al-Qardawi, Y. (1968), Fiqh al Zakah – Comparative Study of Zakah, Regulations and Philosophy in the Light of Qur'an and Sunnah Volume II (Translated), Scientific Publishing Centre King Abdulaziz University, Jeddah, p. 351, available at: http://monzer.kahf.com/books/ english/fiqhalzakah_vol1.pdf (accessed 25 May 2012).

Awojobi, O. and Bein, M.A. (2011), "Microfinancing for poverty reduction and economic development; a case for Nigeria", International Research Journal of Finance and Economics, Vol. 1 No. 72, pp. 159-168.

Azam, M., Iqbal, N., & Tayyab, M. (2014). Zakat and Economic Development: Micro and Macro Level Evidence from Pakistan. Bulletin of Business and Economics (BBE), 3(2), 85–95.

Barrette, A.J. and Beardmore, R.M. (2000), "India's urban poverty agenda: understanding the poor in cities and formulating appropriate anti-poverty actions", a discussion paper for South Asia and City Management Course, Washington, DC.

Baird, K., & Wang, H. (2008). Employee empowerment: extent of adoption and influential factors. Personal Review (Q2), Emerald Group Publishing Limited, 39 (5) p. 574-599.

Bakar, N and Rahman, A "A Comparative Study of Zakah and Modern Taxation" J.KAU: Islamic Econ., Vol. 20, No. 1, pp: 25-40

Bakar, N and Rashid, H. (2010) "Motivations of Paying Zakat on Income: Evidence from Malaysia". International Journal of Economics and Finance, Vol. 2, No. 3; August 2010

Badrudin, R. (2015). Evaluation of The Specific Allocation Fund for Indonesian Society Welfare. International Journal of Applied Business and Economic Research, 13(7), 5609-5626.

Badrudin, R., & Siregar, B. (2015). The evaluation of the implementation of regional autonomy in Indonesia. 1–11.

Bakar, N.B.A. & A. Rahman. (2007). A Comparative Study of Zakah and Modern Taxation. Journal of King Abdul Aziz University: Islamic Economics, Vol. 20 (1): 25-40.

Basu, Kaushik (1984), The Less Developed Economy: A Critique of Contemporary Theory, Basil Blackwell, Oxford.

Beik, I. S., (2009). "Analisis Peran Zakat dalam Mengurangi Kemiskinan: Studi Kasus Dompet Dhuafa Republika [Analysis of Zakat potential in Alleviating Poverty: Case Study of Dompet Dhuafa Republika]". Zakat and Empowering, II. Available at http://imz.or.id/new/uploads/2011/10/Analisis-Peran-Zakat-dalam Mengurangi-Kemiskinan. accessed at April 25th 2012.

Beik etal (2011), Indonesia zakat and development Report 2011, Ciputat, IMZ.

Bourguignon, Francois (2004), "The Poverty-Growth-Inequality Triangle", Paper presented at the Indian Council for Research on International Economic Relations, New Delhi.

Business Independency. International Journal of Nusantara Islam, 5 (01), p. 85-96. Retrieved from https://journal.uinsgd.ac.id/index.php/ijni/article/view/1546.

Chowdhury, Nuimuddin. (1983). Aggregate Demand and Al-Zakah. Thoughts on Economics, Vol. 4, No.9, 1-8.

Conger, J.A. and Kanungo, R.N. (1988) The Empowerment Process: Integrating Theory and Practice. Academy of Management Review, 13, 471-482.

Carney, P. (1992), "The concept of poverty", Public Health Nursing, Vol. 9 No. 2, pp. 74-80.

Carvalho, J.-P. (2009), "A theory of the Islamic revival", available at: http://tuvalu.santafe.edu/Bbowles/TheoryIslamicRevival.pdf (accessed 25 March 2013). Central Intelligence Agency Factbook (2013), "Country Socio-economic data", The online Factbook, Washington, DC.
Chambers, R. (2006), What is Poverty? Who Asks? Who Answers? In Poverty in Focus, UNDP International Poverty Centre, December, available at: www.ipc-undp.org/pub/ IPCPovertyInFocus9.pdf

Cizakca, M. (2004), "Cash Waqf as alternative to NBFIs bank", presentation at the International Seminar on Nonbank Financial Institutions: Islamic Alternatives, jointly organized by Islamic Research and Training Institute, Islamic Development Bank and Islamic Banking and Finance Institute Malaysia, Kuala Lumpur, 1-3 March.

Darwanto, H., 2010. "Pemberdayaan Masyarakat Pedesaan Berbasiskan Masyarakat Terpencil [Villagers Empowerment Based on Remote People]". Available at: www.bappenas.go.id/get-file-server/node/8514/, accessed at November 13th, 2010.

Datt G. and M. Ravallion (1992), "Growth and Redistribution Components of Changes in Poverty Measures: A Decomposition with Application to Brazil and India in the 1980s", Journal of Development Economics, 38, 275-95.

Debnath, Sajit C., Mohammad T. Islam, and Kazi T. Mahmud (2013) The Potential of Zakat Scheme as an Alternative of Microcredit to Alleviate Poverty in Bangladesh. 9th International Conference on Islamic Economics and Finance QFIS, Doha, Qatar.

Dollar, David and Aart Kraay (2002), "Growth is Good for the Poor", Journal of Economic Growth, 7, 195-225.

Doi, I.A. (1990), Shari'ah: The Islamic Law, Ta'ha Publishers, London.

Dusuki, A.W. (2008), "What does Islam say about corporate social responsibility? International association for Islamic economics", Review of Islamic Economics, Vol. 12 No. 1, pp. 5-28.

Fauzia, A. (2013). Faith and the state: A history of Islamic philanthropy in Indonesia (Vol. 1). Brill.

Ferreira, Francisco H.G. (1999), "Inequality and Economic Performance: A Brief Overview to Theories of Growth and Distribution," Text for World Bank's Website on Inequality, Poverty, and Socioeconomic Performance (http://www.worldbank.org/poverty/inequal/index.htm)

Fox, K.S., (1974). Social Indicators and Social Theory : Elements of an Operational System. New York: Wiley.

Fukuda-Parr, S. (2006), The Human Poverty Index: A Multidimensional Measure. In Poverty in Focus, UNDP International Poverty Centre, IPC, UNDP/IPC-IG Brasilia-DE, December, available at: www.ipc-undp.org/pub/IPCPovertyInFocus9.pdf

Gill, S. A., Aftab, R., Rehman, S. U., & Javaid, S. (2018). Youth empowerment and sustainable development An evidence from Pakistan's Prime Minister's Youth

Program. Journal of Economic and Administrative Sciences (Q4), Emerald Group Publishing Limited, p. 1-18.

Green, D. (2015). 1/4 of the world's people already subject to large annual wealth tax to tackle poverty. Has anyone told Piketty?

Guermat,C. T. Al-Utaibi, and J. P. Tucker, (2003). The Practice of Zakat: An Empirical Examination of Four Gulf Countries. Discussion Paper. Exeter University, Department of Economics.

Hairunnizam Wahid & Radiah Abdul Kader (2010), 'Localization of Malaysian zakat distribution: perception of amil and zakat recipients', Proceedings of Seventh International Conference – The Tawhidi Epistemology: Zakat and Waqf Economy.

Hairunnizam Wahid, Sanep Ahmad & Radiah Abdul Kader (2008), 'Pengagihan zakat oleh institusi zakat di Malaysia: mengapa masyarakat Islam tidak berpuas hati', Proceedings of Seminar Kebangsaan Ekonomi Malaysia 2008.

Hamzah. (2017). Empowerment of Mustahiq Zakat Model Towards

Haq, A., Ashraf, M., & Farooq, M. O. (2017). Zakat, Persistence of Poverty and Structural Incidental Segmented Approach: A Survey of Literature.

Hasanuzzaman, S. M. (1976). Zakat and Fiscal Policy, unpublished. Presented at First International Conference on Islamic Economics, Makka.

Hassan, M. Kabir and Jauanyed Masrur Khan (2007) Zakat, External Debt and Poverty Reduction Strategy in Bangladesh. Journal of Economic Cooperation 28:4, 1–38.

Hassan, M. K., & Khan, J. M. (2007). Zakat, external debt and poverty reduction strategy in Bangladesh. Journal of Economic Cooperation, 28(4), 1-38.

Hassan, K. (2010). "An integrated poverty alleviation model combining zakat, awqaf and micro-finance, Seventh International Conference – The Tawhidi Epistemology: Zakat and Waqf Economy, Bangi – Malaysia 2010

Hoque, N., Khan, A., & Mohammad, D. (2015). Poverty alleviation by zakah in transitional economy: A small business entrepreneurial framework. Journal of Global Entrepreneurship Framework, 5(7), 1-20.

Hudaefi, F. A., Zaenal, M. H., Farchatunnisa, H., & Junari, U. L. (2019). How does zakat institution respond to fintech ? Evidence from BAZNAS Indonesia. In Puskas Working Papers.

Hudayati. A. and Tohirin, A. (2010). "Management of zakah: centralised vs decentralised approach", Seventh International Conference – The Tawhidi Epistemology: Zakat and Waqf Economy, Bangi- Malaysia 2010

Husein Sahata. (2003). Muhasabah al Zakah. Mesir, Dar al Syuruq Cairo.

Ibn Abidin, Muhammad Amin (1301H), Hashiyah radd al Muhtar 'ala al Durr al Mukhtar, Istanbul (in Arabic).

Jennings, Medina, M., & McLoughlin. (2006). Toward a Critical Social Theory of Youth Empowerment. Journal of Community Practice (Q2), The Haworth Press, p. 31-55. Available online at http://www.haworthpress.com/web/COM.

Kahf, Monzer, (2006). "Role of Zakat and Awqaf in Reducing Poverty: a Case for Zakat-Awqaf- Based Institutional Setting of Micro-finance", Paper for the Conference on Poverty reduction in the Muslim Countries.

Kahf, M. (1999). The principle of socio-economic justice in the contemporary fiqh of zakat. The Iqtisad, University Islam Indonesia: CIESD

Kakwani, Nanak (1993), "Poverty and Income Growth with Application to Cote d'Ivoire", Review of Income and Wealth, 39, 121-39.

Kar, D. (2007), "Religion and roots of India's caste system", The Washington Post.

Khan, M. A. (1974). Modern Texation and Zakat. Islamic Education, 7 (3), 7-15.

Khan, M.H. (2001), "Rural poverty in developing countries implications for public policy.", Economic Issues No. 26, International Monetary Fund, Washington, DC, available at: www.imf.org/external/pubs/ft/issues/issues26/ (accessed 2 April 2013).

Kasri, Rahmatina A. (2016). "Effectiveness of Zakah Targeting In Alleviating Poverty in Indonesia". Al-Iqtishad:Jurnal Ilmu Ekonomi Syariah (Journal of Islamic Economics) Volume 8 (2), July 2016.

Kuznets, S. (1955), "Economic Growth and Income Inequality", American Economic Review, 45, 1-28.

Lakin, R., & Mahoney, A (2006). Empowering youth to change their world: Identifying key components of a community service program to promote positive development. Journal of School Psychology (Q1), Elsevier, p. 513–531.

Lawton, M.E. et al. (1982). In Lawton, M.P. 1987. Measures of Quality of Life and Subjective Well-being. Generations, Spring 97.

Lawton, M.P. (1987). Measures of Quality of Life and objective Well-being. Generations, Spring.

Lembaga Zakat Selangor (2010), 'Pengertian zakat', Retrieved on February 7th, 2011, from: http://www.e-zakat.com.my/infozakat/pengertian-zakat/

Lewis, W. Arthur (1954), "Economic Development with Unlimited Supply of Labour', Manchester School, 22, pp.139-191.

Lucas, R. (1988), "On the Mechanics of Economic Development", Journal of Monetary Economics, 22, 3-42.

Luttrell, C., S. Quiroz, C. Scrutton, and K. Bird, 2009. "Understanding and Operationalising Empowerment". Overseas Development Institute. Working Paper 308; Results of ODI research presented in preliminary form for discussion and critical comment. Available at http://www.idra.it/garnetpapers/C07Tanim_Laila.pdf. accessed on April 24th 2012.

M. Akram, Mian and M. Afzal (2014) Dynamic Role of Zakat in Alleviating Poverty: A Case Study of Pakistan. University Library of Munich, Germany.

Malik, B. A. (2016). Philanthropy in Practice: Role of Zakat in the Realization of Justice and Economic Growth. International Journal of Zakat, 1(1), 64–77.

Mannan, M. A. (1986), Islamic Economics: Theory and Practices, Cambridge: Hodder and Stroughton.

Mannan. M.A (1989).Effects of Zakah Assessment and Collection on the Redistribution of Income in Contemporary Muslim Countries.

Mohamed Dahan Abdul Latif 1998, 'Zakat management and administration in Malaysia', Proceedings of Seminar of Zakat and Taxation.

Muhammad, S., & Saad, R. (2016). The Impact of Public Governance Quality, Accountability, and Effectiveness on Intention to Pay Zakat: Moderating Effect of Trust on Zakat Institutions. International Journal of Management Research & Review, 6(1), 1-8.

Mannan, M. Abdul, (1989). Ekonomi Islam: Teoti dan Praktis. Jil 1. Kuala Lumpur: A.S. Noordeen.

Maslow, A. (1954). Toward a Psychology of Being. New York: van Nostran.

Mohd Parid Shaikh Ahmad, (2001). Kaedah Pengagihan Dana Zakat: Satu Perspektif Islam (edited by Nik

Mohsin, M.I.A. (2013), "Potential of Zakat in eliminating Riba in and eradicating Muslim countries", EJBM-Special Issue: Islamic Management and Business, Vol. 5 No. 11, pp. 114-126.

Mohajer, N. & Earnest, J. (2009). Youth empowerment for the most vulnerable: A model based on the pedagogy of Freire and experiences in the field). Health Education (Q2), Emerald Group Publishing Limited, 109 (5) p. 424-438.

Morduch, J., Hashemi, S. and Littlefield, E. (2003), "Is microfinance an effective strategy to reach the Millennium Development Goal?", CGAP working paper, Focus Note 24, Washington, DC.

Muhamat, A. A., Jaafar, N., Rosly, H. E. & Manan, H. A. (2013). An appraisal on the business success of entrepreneurial asnaf. An empirical study on the state zakat organization (the Selangor Zakat Board or Lembaga Zakat Selangor) in Malaysia. Journal of Financial Reporting and Accounting, 11 (1), p. 51-63.

Murrel and Norris., (1983). Assessing health and human Service Needs: Concept, Method and Applications. New York: Human Science Press.

Muslehuddin, M. (1970). Commenwealth of Islamic Countries and the Muslim World Bank. The Criterion.

Mustofa al-Khin, Mustofa al-Bugho (Dr.), Ali al-Syarbaji, (2005). Fiqh Mazhab Syafie, Kuala Lumpur, Pustaka Salam.

Nadzri, F. A. A. et.al. (2012). Zakah and Poverty Alleviation: Roles of Zakah Institutions in Malaysia, International Journal of Arts and Commerce, Vol. 1, No.7: 61-72.

Qadri, S. A. (1963). Provident Funad ki Zakat ka Masalah (Zakat on Provident Funad), (Urdu), Zindgi, 30 (2), 43-59.

Qaradawi, Yusuf al (1999) Fiqh az-Zakat: A Comparative Study—The Rules, Regulations and Philosophy of Zakat in the Light of the Qur'an and Sunnah. Dar Al Taqwa Ltd. London.

Pailis, E A., Burhan, U., Multifiah, & Ashar, K. (2016). The Influence of Maqashid Syariah Toward Mustahik's Empowerment and Welfare (Study of Productive Zakat Recipients on BAZNAS Riau). American Journal of Economics, 6 (2), 39-59.

Pollard, J., Datta, K., James, A., & Akli, Q. (2015). Islamic charitable infrastructure and giving in East London: Everyday economic-development geographies in practice. Journal of Economic Geography, 16(4), 871–896.

Pramanik, A. H. (2002). Islam and development revisited with evidence from Malaysia. Islamic Economic Studies, 10(1), 39-74

Pramanik, Ataul Huq. (1998). Pembangunan dan Pengagihan dalam Islam. Kuala Lumpur: Dewan Bahasa dan Pustaka.

Puskas BAZNAS. (2020). Outlook Zakat Indonesia 2020. In Baznas.

Rahman, Afzalur. (2002). Dokrin Ekonomi Islam Jilid 3, Yogyakarta: Dana Bhakti Prima Yasa.

Rahim, S., & Hanani, K. (2014). An Economic Research on Zakat Compliance Among Muslim's Staff in Unimas. International Conference on Masjid, Zakat, and Waqf, 53-65. Kuala Lumpur.

Raimi, L. and Mobolaji, H.I. (2008), "Imperative of economic integration among Muslim countries: lessons from European globalisation", Humanomics, Vol. 24 No. 2, pp. 130-144.

Ramli, R.M. et.al. (2011). Understanding asnaf attitude: Malaysia's experience in quest for an effective Zakah distribution programme. In International Zakah Conference: Sustainable Zakah Development in the Poverty Alleviation and Improvement of Welfare of the Ummah.

Rao, J. (2010), "The caste system: effects on poverty in India", Global Majority E-Journal, Vol. 1 No. 2, pp. 97-106.

Raquib, A. (2011). Islamic Banking & Zakah-An Alternative Approach to Poverty Reduction in Bangladesh. Journal of Islamic Economics, Banking and Finance, 7(2): 11-26

Rashidah, R and Awang, R. (2003). "Assessing Business Zakat at Pusat Zakat Selangor: Between Theory and Practice", Journal of Financial Reporting and Accounting, Vol. 1 Issue: 1, pp.33 – 48

Ravallion, M. (2005), "A comparative perspective on poverty reduction in Brazil, China and India", Research Working Paper No. 5080, The World Bank, Washington, DC, available at: www.economist.com/node/14979330 (accessed May 2013).

Riyadi, Agus. (2014). Manajemen Pengelolaan Zakat Produktif dalam Perspektif Bank Islam. Iqtishadia, 7 (2), 335 – 356.

Rohim, A. N. (2019). Optimalisasi penghimpunan zakat melalui digital fundraising. Al-Balagh : Jurnal Dakwah Dan Komunikasi, 4(1), 59.

Romer, P. M. (1986), "Increasing Returns and Long-run Growth", Journal of Political Economy, 94, 1002-37.

Salama, Abdin Ahmed (1982), "Fiscal Analysis of Zakat with Special Reference to Saudi Arabia's Experience in Zakat", in Mohammad Ariff (Editor), Monetary and Fiscal Policy of Islam, International Centre for Research in Islamic Economics, King Abdul Aziz University, Jeddah, 341-64

Saleem, A. M. (2014). Understanding the role of 'Zakat' in humanitarian response. Retrieved from http://devinit.org/post/understanding-role-zakat-humanitarian-response

Sadeq, A.H.M., (1987). "Economic Growth in an Islamic Economy. Conference paper in International Seminar on Islamic Economics, Kuliyyah Economics, UIAM.

Sahroni, O., Setiawan, A., Suharsono, M. & Setiawan, A. (2019). Fikih Zakat Kontemporer. Depok: Rajawali Pres.

Sanep Ahmad, Hairunnizam Wahid & Adnan Mohamad (2006), 'Penswastaan institusi zakat dan kesannya terhadap pembayaran secara

Santoso, I. R. (2019). Strategy for optimizing zakat digitalization in alleviation poverty in the era of industrial revolution 4.0. Ikonomika, 4(1), 35–52.

Sarea, A. (2012). Zakat as a Benchmark to Evaluate Economic Growth: An Alternative Approach. International Journal of Business and Social Science, 3(18), 242-245.

Sartika, M., 2008. "Pengaruh Pendayagunaan Zakat Produktif terhadap Pemberdayaan Mustahik pada LAZ Yayasan Solo Peduli Surakarta [Effect of Productive Zakat's Empowerment toward Mustahik Empowerment at LAZ Solo Peduli Foundation, Surakarta]". Jurnal Ekonomi Islam La_Riba, II (1), 79-89.

Shaikh, S. A. (2016). Zakat Collectible in OIC Countries for Poverty Alleviation: A Primer on Empirical Estimation. International Journal of Zakat, 1(1), 17–35.

Shirazi, Nasim S. (2014) Integrating Zakat and Waqf into the Poverty Reduction Strategy of the IDB Member Countries. Islamic Economic Studies 22:1, 79–108.

Shirazi, N. S. (2014). Integrating Zakat and Waqf into the Poverty Reduction Strategy of the IDB Member Countries. Islamic Economic Studies, 22(1), 79-108.

Siddiqi, S. A. (1968), Public Finance in Islam, S. H. Muhammad Ashraf, Lahore, Pakistan.

Siddiqi, M.N. (1988), "The Guarantee of a Minimum Level of Living in an Islamic State", in Munawar Iqbal (Editor), Distributive Justice and Need Fulfillment in an Islamic Economy, The Islamic Foundation, Leicester, 251-86.

Siddiqi, M.N. (1988), "The Guarantee of a Minimum Level of Living in an Islamic State", in Munawar Iqbal (Editor), Distributive Justice and Need Fulfillment in an Islamic Economy, The Islamic Foundation, Leicester, 251-86.

Soetomo. (2015). Pemberdayaan Masyarakat. Yogyakarta: Pustaka Pelajar.

Stirk, C. (2015). An Act of Faith: Humanitarian Financing of Zakat.

Syed Othman al Habshi, (1990). Peranan dan Struktur Bayt al Mal, Zakat dan Wakaf Di Dalam Konteks Peralihan Arah Strategi Pembangunan Ekonomi Umat

Islam, Paper presented at the Seminar On Islam and Development organized by IIUM.

Syamsuri. (2018). Ekonomi Pembangunan Islam, Sebuah Prinsip, Konsep dan Asas Falsafahnya. Ponorogo: UNIDA Gontor Press. Undang-Undang No. 40 Tahun 2009 tentang Kepemudaan.

Syahrullah & Ulfah, M. (2016). The response of Indonesian Academicians toward Factors Influencing the Payment of Zakat on Employment Income. Research on Humanities and Social Sciences, .6(10), 87-94.

Syed Othman Al Habshi, (2006). Peranan Zakat Dalam Membantu Pembangunan Ekonomi Negara

Syukri Salleh (Prof. Dr.)2006, Lokalisasi Zakat (edited by Abdul Ghafar Ismail and Hailani Muji Tahir 2006,) in Zakat, Persyariatan Perekonomian dan Perundangan, Bangi UKM.

Tampubolon, J. Basita GS, Margono. S, Djoko S & Sumardjo. S.(2006). Community Empowerment through a Group Approach (Case of Empowering the Poor Through a Business Group Approach (KUBE). Journal penyuluhan. Vol. 2 No. 2 (2006). http://jurnal.ipb.ac.id/index.php/jupe/article/view/2122

The Nation (2013), "44pc of poverty-hit live in Muslim countries", available at www.nation.com.pk/pakistan-news-newspaper-daily-english-online/business/25-Apr-2011/44pc-of-   povertyhit--live-in-Muslim-countries (accessed 29 July 2013).

Todaro, M.P. and Smith, S.C. (2012), Economic Development, 11th ed., Pearson Education Inc.

Townsend, P. (2006), What is Poverty? An Historical Perspective. In Poverty in Focus, UNDP International Poverty Centre, December, available at: www.ipc-undp.org/pub/ IPCPovertyInFocus9.pdf

United Nations Millennium Declaration (2000), Millennium Development Goals, Vol. 55, No. 2, United Nations General Assembly Resolution, New York, NY, available at: www.un.org/ millennium/declaration/ares552e.pdf (accessed 3 April 2013).

Wahbah al Zuhaili, (2005). Usul al Fiqh al Islami, Dar al Fikr Damsyiq.

Wali, H. N. (2013). Utilization of Zakat and Islamic Endowment Funds for Poverty Reduction: A Case Study of Zakat and Hubsi Commission, Kano State-Nigeria. Journal of Economics and Sustainable Development, 4(18), 141–147.

World Bank (1999), World Development Report 1998/99: Knowledge and Development, Oxford University Press, New York.

Yusoff, Mohammed B. (2011) Zakat Expenditure, School Enrolment, and Economic Growth in Malaysia. International Journal of Business and Social Science 2:6, 175–181.

Yusuf Qardhawi (2000), Fiqh al-Zakah, English Translation by Monzer Kahf, Jeddah, Scientific Publishing Centre, King Abdul Aziz University.

Zaenal, M. H., Astuti, A. D., & Sadariyah, A. S. (2018). Increasing urban community empowerment through changing of poverty rate index on the productive zakat impact. IOP Conf. Series: Earth and Environmental Science 106. P. 1-

Zayas, F. G. (2003), The Law and Institution of Zakat, Kuala Lumpur: The Other Press.

Printed by Books on Demand GmbH, Norderstedt / Germany